TRAVIS CUSHMAN

CHILD
ABUSE
AND
NEGLECT
CASES

A Comprehensive Guide to
Understanding the System

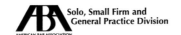
Solo, Small Firm and
General Practice Division
AMERICAN BAR ASSOCIATION

Cover design by Elmarie Jara/ABA Design

Printed in the United States of America.

20 19 18 17 16   5 4 3 2 1

ISBN: 978-1-63425-590-5

e-ISBN: 978-1-63425-591-2

Discounts are available for books ordered in bulk. Special consideration is given to state bars, CLE programs, and other bar-related organizations. Inquire at Book Publishing, ABA Publishing, American Bar Association, 321 N. Clark Street, Chicago, Illinois 60654-7598.

www.shopABA.org

CONTENTS

PRELUDE

Introduction   1
  Story: College Bound   1
  A Need for a "Working" System   2
  Story: 75 years   3
The "System"   4
  Terms and Definitions   4
  Federal System/State Systems/Local Support Providers   5
  The Need for a Balanced and Neutral System   7
Inherent Biases   7
  Disparity in Resources   8
  System Repercussions/High Turnover Rate   9
Personal Biases   10
  People Want to Protect Children/All Care Providers Wear White Hats   11
  Presumption of Guilt   13
Avoidable Biases   13
  Petition Filing/Contract Attorneys   14
  Guardian Ad Litem   16
  Child Protection Specialist   17
Ombudsman   18
All Parties Must Drive the Bus   19
Purpose of This Guide   20

SECTIONS
Introduction to the Sections   21

SECTION 1
Receiving an Initial Report and Assigning a CPS   23
  Checklist: Receiving a Report – Possible Abuse or Neglect   25

SECTION 2
Danger Assessment – To Remove or Not to Remove   27
  Checklist: Danger Assessment – To Remove or Not to Remove   29

SECTION 3
Comprehensive Family Functioning Assessment   33
  Checklist: Child Safety Assessment   35
  Checklist: Parenting Assessment and Family Functioning   37

SECTION 4
TIA vs. TLC   41
Checklist: TIA vs TLC – Advantages and Disadvantages   44

SECTION 5
Drafting an Affidavit in Support of a Court Petition   47
Checklist: CPS Affidavit in Support of a Court Petition   49

SECTION 6
Drafting and Filing a Petition with the Court   51
Checklist: State's Petition for Court Intervention   53

SECTION 7
Show Cause Hearing   55
Bench Card: Show Cause Hearing   58

SECTION 8
Mediation   61
Checklist: Mediation   66

SECTION 9
Adjudication Hearing   69
Bench Card: Adjudication Hearing   72

SECTION 10
Dispositional Hearing – Treatment Plan   75
Bench Card: Dispositional Hearing   78

SECTION 11
Status Hearing/Review Hearing   81
Bench Card: Status/Review Hearing   83

SECTION 12
Extension of Temporary Legal Custody   85
Bench Card: Extension of TLC Hearing   87

SECTION 13
Permanency Plan   89

SECTION 14
Permanency Hearing   91
Bench Card: Permanency Plan Hearing   93

SECTION 15
Hearing to Dismiss/Reunify   95
Bench Card: Dismissal Hearing   97

SECTION 16
Voluntary Relinquishment Hearing   99
Bench Card: Relinquishment Hearing   101

SECTION 17
Guardianship Hearing   103
Bench Card: Guardianship Hearing   105

SECTION 18
Termination of Parental Rights   107
Bench Card: Termination Hearing   109

SECTION 19
Notice of Appeal/Appealing   111

POSTLUDE
Roles of Parties Before and During Hearings   113
Children in the Courtroom   119
ICWA, Additional Requirements   120

PDFs of the checklists and bench cards can be downloaded from http://ambar.org/childabuse.

INTRODUCTION

Story: College Bound

The affidavit drafted by the child protection specialist in support of removing the children from their birth mother stated the teenage girl was admitted to the hospital for attempting suicide by slitting her wrist. The girl, the oldest of three half-siblings, had no friends, was failing in school and had fallen into a state of depression, a mood in which she could see no way out. Because she did not know how to escape her current lifestyle, she tried to end her own life, a cry for help.

The life she no longer wanted to live was one filled with abuse and neglect by her mother and stepfather. The mostly verbal abuse occurred frequently and was a result of her mother and stepfather's alcohol and drug addictions. Their addictions also forced the young girl to care for her two younger half-siblings on a day-to-day basis.

The teenager seemed more mature than many adults. She never had the chance to be a child. Despite this, she loved her mother and hoped her mother would get help. She also did not want herself or her half-siblings to continue living their current lifestyle. She thought about it long and hard and concluded that she could no longer live with the one person she loved the most, her mother. So the young girl slit her wrist, which in turn got the attention of the local Child and Family Services Office.

After the children were removed from their home, they were placed with their maternal grandfather. The children were familiar with this setting since they had spent many nights there because their own home usually lacked food, heat, and at times running water.

From the beginning of the case, the girl struggled with the uncertainty of being reunited with her mother. She also struggled with the fact that her half-siblings might have to go back and live the old lifestyle again. She knew that she could not abandon them, so if they went back, she would have to go back just to protect them. She cried often.

As the case proceeded through the court system, her parents fought the court-imposed changes. Although her parents were fighting the changes, her anxiety subsided since she knew something was being done by her court-appointed attorney. While living at her grandfather's house, she was able to sleep through the night, was making new friends, and was improving her school performance.

The parties involved in the case worked collectively and diligently to rehabilitate the parents while the children were protected and properly cared for in a kinship placement. The goal of reunification, however, became unrealistic and before the end of the case, her mother voluntarily relinquished her rights and the maternal grandparents were granted guardianship over the three children.

The teenager's grades began to reflect the change. She went from failing in school to earning "A's" in all subjects. She graduated from high school early and was awarded an academic scholarship to attend college. Her life changed for the better because the child protection system in the community where she lived was working as designed.

The system worked because it was neutral and balanced. It protected the children while trying to rehabilitate the parents. The children's mother eventually beat her addiction and reunited herself with the ones she loved the most, her family.

A Need for a "Working" System

America's children are our most important assets. For some of them, their future is in our hands. These children, the ones who need the child protection system to work, typically live in environments that include substance abuse, domestic violence, and poor living conditions. Many are from families living in poverty and often have little extended family support. As such, these children are seldom taught the benefits of having a good education, a hard work ethic, and addiction avoidance.

These vulnerable children often become truant at school or drop out before they graduate. As they mature, the children often develop social, emotional, and cognitive impairment.[1] They indulge in health-risk behaviors and tend to resort to violence rather than communication to settle disagreements with their peers, parents, and other family members. They may become runaways or worse, juvenile felons.

A working system, is a child protection system whose intervention strategies, policies, practices, and programs are working properly so that it protects the children while also helping their parents. A good state child protection system has a vast network of evidence-based services to treat child victims and potentially rehabilitate and educate the parents. Child victims benefit by receiving help with their emotions and learning behavioral tools and lifestyle choices that can improve their mental health.

A working system includes collaboration with local, state, and national agencies to give children the opportunity to change and improve. Without a working system that incorporates community help and other governmental

---

[1] The Adverse Childhood Experiences Study, http://www.acestudy.org.

support, many of these children will grow up to parent in the same manner as their parents. Statistical data shows that children who grow up as victims of abuse or neglect have a greater chance of becoming abusers.[2] For this reason, as well as many more, it is in our society's best interest to stop this cycle of abuse and neglect.

Stopping the cycle of abuse and neglect is important for citizens and taxpayers. It's vital to increasing a community's overall health and also reducing the burden on the state in caring for these victims when they are adults. Stopping the cycle and properly caring for children in need also prevents incarceration as the next story illustrates.

Story: 75 years

The newspaper's headline read: "Teen gets 75 years."[3] The judge sentenced a 15-year-old boy to 75 years in prison after the boy pleaded guilty to raping a neighbor girl while the two were walking home from school.

Family members, friends and professionals who testified at the boy's sentencing hearing all explained how the boy was slapped, hit, kicked, and locked in closets by his mother who raised him until he was ten years of age. They testified how the boy had little to no guidance and was often sent to school unclean. "She was just cruel," testified the boy's paternal grandmother. His emotional maturity was two or three years less than his chronological age, according to the administrator of the youth detention center.

"It is terribly unfortunate that the boy's life went so wrong so early," stated the sentencing judge. The child's attorney argued he was a "broken boy" and could be a "poster child for a kid who fell through the cracks in the system."

The opinion that the child protective system failed the boy was echoed by many. Others went even further and said they believed the system not only failed the boy, but also failed the girl who now would have to learn how to live as a rape survivor. Many in the community felt that had its child protection system worked properly, the cycle of abuse would have been broken, thereby saving both children.

The community will never know if a properly working child protective system could have prevented this incident. What is known, unfortunately, is that the boy's learned behavior pattern was taught to him early in life. The factual events of this young boy's life show why the cycle of abuse must be broken before a community can become truly healthy. To accomplish this task, the child protection system must take a multigenerational approach and both rehabilitate and educate parents to break the cycle of abuse in raising their children.

---

[2] Continuing the cycle of abuse, http://www.safehorizon.org/page/child-abuse-facts-56.html (estimated that one-third of abused and neglected children will grow up to abuse their own children).

[3] *Teen Gets 75 Years*, Great Falls Tribune, December 12, 2013.

THE "SYSTEM"

All 50 states, the District of Columbia, the Commonwealth of Puerto Rico, and the Virgin Islands have child protection systems.[4] The "System," as referred to throughout the remainder of this guide, is a generic term that stands for a state's department or division and its supporting agencies and organizations that collectively keep children safe and families strong by addressing the abuse and neglect reports.

The System is not limited to any one state's system. Many state systems have a different name, acronym or abbreviation sequence for their respective state agency. They may also be organized differently and/or their parts may operate independently. They all do, however, serve the same function: to protect children. Along with understanding this book's definition of the word System, the reader should also be familiar with other terms and definitions that are being used in this guide.

Terms and Definitions

- DPHHS (Department of Public Health and Human Services), a state department that oversees and/or administers programs aimed at helping the health of the state's general public population.

- CFS (Child and Family Services Division), an agency within a state's DPHHS that concentrates on protecting the state's children from being abused and neglected.

- CPS (Child Protection Specialist), a social worker who is employed by CFS who works directly with abused children and their parents to protect the children and rehabilitate the parents.

- TIA (Temporary Investigative Authority), a court order that gives the DPHHS/CFS temporary authority over the subject child and the child's parents for the reason of formally investigating allegations of abuse and neglect.

- TLC (Temporary Legal Custody), a court order that gives the DPHHS/CFS temporary legal custody over the subject child and authorizes the state to mandate services for the child's parents for the purpose of formally protecting the child from any further abuse or neglect while the parents work through programs aimed at rehabilitating the parents and/or teaching them parenting skills to reunify with the child safely.

In addition to the terms and definitions printed above there will be additional acronyms and abbreviations throughout the guide's chapters. All of

---

[4] *The Child Welfare System*, http://www.firststar.org/library/child-welfare-system-overview.aspx.

these should help the flow of reading and understanding of the System, both state and federal.

Federal System/State Systems/Local Support Providers

The "System" is complex at both the federal and state levels. The U.S. Department of Health and Human Services is comprised of over 64,000 employees with an annual budget of over 700 billion dollars.[5] The federal system, as we know it, dates back to 1974 when the U.S. government began taking a leadership role in seeing that children are cared for properly. The federal government took on this role after passage of the Child Abuse Prevention and Treatment Act (CAPTA).[6]

Congress enacted CAPTA to protect children in the wake of national awareness of the escalating number of children being abused or neglected by their parents. When these high-profile cases began making national headlines and demonstrating the prevalence of physical abuse, mental neglect, and sexual abuse occurrence, CAPTA was enacted.

Congress has amended CAPTA several times, including through the CAPTA Reauthorization Act of 2010.[7] CAPTA still governs legislation but the federal government's original legislative intent has been modified several times.

The first modification came six years after CAPTA's enactment, in response to the substantial increase in children residing in foster care homes. The increase in care inherently increased foster care costs.[8] These increases prompted Congress to pass the Adoption Assistance and Child Welfare Act of 1980 (AACWA).[9] AACWA intended to preserve families and thereby reduce the number of children in foster care homes.

By the mid-1990s, critics of the "family preservation" system became increasingly outspoken. As a result, Congress shifted away from the family reunification ideology by passing another act that made "child safety" its top priority.[10] This act, adopted by Congress in 1997, was titled the Adoption and Safe Families Act (ASFA).[11] ASFA is still the current law that governs HHS's policies and procedures. Although ASFA did not eliminate the family

---

[5] www.whistleblowers.org/press-room/in-the-news/1147-grassley-outlines-challenges-facing-next-health-human-services-secretary

[6] Child Abuse Prevention and Treatment Act of 1974, Pub. L. No. 93-247 (1974); *see also* http://www.gpo.gov/fdsys/pkg/STATUTE-88/pdf/STATUTE-88-Pg4.pdf; or http://uscode.house.gov/download/download.shtml.

[7] About CAPTA: A Legislative History by the Child Welfare Information Gateway (2011).

[8] Kathy Barbell and Madelyn Freudnlich, *Foster Care Today* (2001).

[9] Adoption Assistance and Child Welfare Act of 1980, Pub. L. No. 96-272 (1980); *see also* http://uscode.house.gov/statutes/1980/1980-096-0272.pdf.

[10] Viki Klee, *NRCFCPP Information Packet: ASFA* (2002); *see also* http://www.hunter.cuny.edu/socwork/nrcfcpp/downloads/information_packets/asfa-pkt.pdf.

[11] *Adoption and Safe Families Act of 1997*, Pub. L. No. 105-89 (1997); *see also* http://www.gpo.gov/fdsys/pkg/PLAW-105publ89/html/PLAW-105publ89.htm.

preservation concept, it did reduce the practice by creating timelines for reunification and termination. ASFA made child safety the primary concern.

ASFA requires that a social worker either reunify the child with his/her parents or terminate the parental rights within a strict time period.[12] If this is not accomplished, individual states will lose federal money and face paying fines.[13] Federal money is granted to the states via CAPTA and under part E of title IV of the Social Security Act. This Act has also been amended including changes made by the passing of the Fostering Connections to Success and Increasing Adoptions Act of 2008.[14] Further funding changes to protect children in foster care occurred in 2014 when the Congress enacted a bipartisan bill titled Preventing Sex Trafficking and Strengthening Families Act.[15] These federal laws are just a few, but not all, of the statutes that comprise the federal system and help shape the many different state systems.

Every state has enacted statutes to address the protection of children. Many states, with some variation, have laws that specify how reports will be investigated and outline procedures for handling confirmed cases of abuse or neglect. Some states have delegated these tasks to individual counties. Additionally, all 50 states have created foster care systems for housing children who are removed from their parents.

These varying state systems, even those in states with relatively low populations, are complex. The many different outside support agencies and organizations that provide services to safeguard the welfare of children compounds the complexity.

Every child protection system requires assistance from other governmental agencies, non-profit organizations, and for-profit companies. This includes city and county peace officers, county attorneys, state attorneys, parents' attorneys, children's attorneys, foster parents and foster parent services, guardians, guardian ad litems and guardian ad litem organizations, licensed youth care facilities, licensed child placing agencies, child-care facilities, health professionals, mental health professionals, state advocacy and protection programs, adoptive parents, juvenile probation and parole, evaluation and research centers, school officials and ICWA experts, as well as other tribal and federal enclaves.

The participants working in this area need to understand and respect its complexity without being confused by it. Participants must safeguard the System so it remains neutral and balanced. One way to avoid becoming

---

[12] J.E.B. MYERS, A SHORT HISTORY OF CHILD PROTECTION IN AMERICA (2008); available at www.americanbar .org/content /dam/aba/.../ChildProtectionHistory.pdf.

[13] 45 C.F.R. § 1356.86 (2012); *see also* http://www.gpo.gov/fdsys/pkg/CFR-2012-title45-vol4/pdf/CFR-2012-title45-vol4-sec1356-86.pdf.

[14] Fostering Connections to Success and Increasing Adoptions Act of 2008, http://www.childwelfare.gov/ topics/systemwide/laws-policies/federal/fosteringconnections.

[15] Preventing Sex Trafficking and Strengthening Families Act, http:// www.congress.gov/bill/113th-congress/house-bill/4980/text

confused by the System is to fully understand why it must remain balanced and neutral.

The Need for a Balanced and Neutral System

Any child protection system will lose efficiency, credibility and cooperation by participants if it is not neutral and balanced. As the founders understood, a successful government requires checks and balances. Similarly, Systems must have checks and balances to help ensure neutrality. When a System remains neutral so that no one part of it has more power than the other parts, the System can work successfully for many years.

But if the complex System created to protect our most vulnerable citizens fails to remain neutral, both the vulnerable children and their parents suffer. This trickles down to immediate families, extended families and communities. Conversely, when a System's checks and balances keep the System free of biases, children are protected, some parents are rehabilitated and other parents' rights are terminated. These results are achieved when experienced and caring judges, prosecuting attorneys, CPS, parents' attorneys, children's attorneys, and guardian ad litems all know their case and have realistic goals regarding the parents' ability to change. Realistic goals can be achieved in most cases when all parties work to support the parents in completing their respective treatment plans while protecting the children.

When a System is working well, it is civil and rewarding for the parties who practice within it. Practicing in the System is rewarding when the parties make a positive difference benefiting both the children and their parents. To keep a System neutral the participants should understand Inherent Biases, Personal Biases and Avoidable Biases. Understanding these three different biases will help one further understand the complexity of the System.

INHERENT BIASES

The first set of biases, biases which cannot be eliminated, are inherent biases. No matter what the governmental system was designed for, protecting children, prosecuting juveniles, or housing adult convicts, it will contain inherent biases that will affect how it operates. Inherent biases refers to the effect of underlying factors or assumptions that skew viewpoints of a subject under discussion.[16]

How quickly the underlying factors or assumptions affect the respective system, and to what degree, ultimately depends on how the system was designed, its size and how many other biases are working against it. To what extent inherent biases affect a system also partially depends on whether the system's participants can recognize the inherent biases affecting that system. Participants in a system must remember that even the best designed system can

---

[16] Inherent bias as defined in Wikipedia.org, The Free Encyclopedia (2 June 2016).

lose its neutral balance because of inherent biases that change the system's efficiency and effectiveness.

Some of the biases in the System designed to protect children are the disparity in resources, system repercussions, and the high turnover rate of court participants in this area of law.

Disparity in Resources

In the System, the state and its supporting care providers typically have more city, county, state and/or federal funding than do the agencies defending the parents.[17] Similarly, they also have more opportunities to receive additional money so they can offer higher pay, training, and continuing education programs.[18]

The State of Montana Office of Public Defender (OPD), the organization responsible for appointing attorneys to defend parents, summed up the disparity of resources when it circulated the following:

> The state is represented by county attorneys who receive competitive salaries and benefits, have supervision, are provided training, and who have the cooperation and assistance of Child and Family Services personnel, including social workers, counselors and therapists, and the active assistance of law enforcement. Reports of suspected abuse or neglect are often generated by persons of perceived high credibility, such as law enforcement officers, medical personnel, and teachers.

> OPD staff attorneys work under heavy caseloads, with inadequate compensation. … OPD lacks adequate investigative staff, has no social worker staff, and has no protocol for the utilization of experts in civil cases. There appears not to be a protocol for obtaining discovery from the prosecution. A staff attorney who handles a large DN [dependent neglect] caseload told me that she spends lengthy periods of time copying file materials from the county attorney's file.[19]

This statement summarizes the depth of disparity in resources within just one state's System. It occurs in many other state's Systems around our nation.[20]

---

[17] Ian Millhiser, (March 18, 2013), public-defenders-hit-up-to-six-times-harder-than-prosecutors-bysequester; *seealso*http://thinkprogress.org/justice/2013/03/18/1725691/public-defenders-hit-up-to-six-times-harder-than-prosecutors-bysequester/.

[18] *Id.*

[19] Proposal to Revise OPD's Dependent/Neglect Program, Public Defender Commission Meeting, (February 15, 2013), http://publicdefender.mt.gov/meetings/docs/02152013/RevisedDNProgram.pdf.

[20] Understanding the comparison of budgets for prosecutors and budgets for public defense, National Legal Aid and Defender Association, (2011), http://www.nlada.net/library/article/na_understandingbudgetsforprosanddefs.

The disparity in resources increases when the defense is on a predetermined budget, which is usually the case.

Agencies defending parents in the child protection system often work within a budget for a predetermined time frame.[21] Thus, the available money is based on an estimate of expense needs. When budgets are determined in advance and funding does not follow the opening of a case, the agency responsible for defending parents may fall behind when more cases than expected are opened. This furthers the disparity in resources between the prosecution and defense in System cases.

An agency responsible for defending parents in System cases must be adequately funded for the attorneys to properly litigate the case against the organization prosecuting the case. If the revenue spent by the state to prosecute System cases increases, so must the amount of money available for the defense of the parents.

Disparity in resources is inherent in many Systems. Participants must be aware of it to help prevent the System from becoming out of balance and losing its neutrality. Disparity in resources can also contribute to other inherent biases like System repercussions and high turnover rates.

System Repercussions/High Turnover Rate

Professionals who work within the System may inadvertently subject themselves to repercussions from other System participants. The repercussions may come from other professional care providers within their community, other organizations assisting in the care of abused or neglected children and/or directly from CFS. An attorney, doctor, counselor, foster parent or guardian ad litems (GALs), who zealously fights the opinions of CFS on a regular basis may feel repercussions from CPS, the participants' contemporaries, and/or care support organizations.

For example, the attorney who vigorously cross-examines a respected doctor or counselor may be treated differently by the doctor when the attorney brings his/her child to see the doctor for a medical exam. Some say this is a given in any legal field while others feel it is more prevalent in System cases. Parents often cannot afford to hire their own experts so they are left to vigorously cross-examine the state's experts, which exacerbates the potential repercussions. Although this bias is more prevalent with attorneys who represent parents, it also occurs with children's attorneys and CFS prosecutors.

Repercussions from other organizations typically surface when the professional seeks the assistance of an organization that has been previously offended. This same sort of repercussion and lack of cooperation may also be felt

---

[21] Montana Public Defender Commission Memo, Harry Freebourn, (May 29, 2015), http://publicdefender .mt.gov/2017BienniumFunding.pdf.

by the professional when working a future case with CFS. When this occurs, children and parents suffer. System repercussions can occur from many different sources during a case and often the professional being victimized by the repercussions may not understand why.

For these reasons, all parties should try to recognize whether repercussions are occurring. They are destructive to the neutrality of the System and also lead to other inherent biases like a high turnover rate.

The disparity in resources between the prosecution and defense, along with the different forms of possible repercussions, can contribute to another inherent bias: increased turnover rate. The turnover rate of employees and volunteers in System cases is higher than average.[22] Protecting children who are victims of abuse and neglect and rehabilitating their parents is not easy for any of the System participants.

System participants bear the burden of absorbing or blocking out many different emotions of their clients, most of which are negative in nature, painful in description and hard to forget. Many participants leave the System after they gain some experience, leading to a higher than normal turnover rate. That is, even though working in the System is mentally stressful, it is also a good place for young professionals to gain court experience. Often they tend to leave the System when their experience level allows them to apply for better jobs.

These are just a few of the inherent biases that may be affecting the balance of a state's child protection system. Along with inherent biases, a person practicing in the System should also be aware of, and look out for, the many different personal biases that can also affect it.

PERSONAL BIASES

In the System, personal biases include, but are not limited to, the presumption that all parents are guilty and that all care providers in the System are there to do the right thing. Personal biases, like inherent biases, affect the System's neutrality. A personal bias can be defined as one's own preconceived opinion about something or someone. Personal biases differ from inherent biases in that they are rooted individually although they may be shared collectively by the other participants. Personal biases are usually system-specific but at times can overlap between different systems.

The first step in controlling a system's personal biases and helping it remain neutral is recognizing and understanding the personal biases. Some of the personal biases one should be aware of within the System are the presumption of guilt, the "White Hat" perception projected toward the professional care providers and the rooted desire to protect children.

---

[22] Turnover in Child Welfare, www.practicenotes.org/vol4_no3.htm.

People Want to Protect Children/All Care Providers Wear White Hats

Most people want to protect children. This mental characteristic exists in most adults even when the children are not descendants or a related family member. Human nature dictates protecting those who do not have the ability to protect themselves.

Most people would rather err on the side of protecting children than see them hurt. This means they would rather see children prematurely removed from their parents than allow the children to possibly be harmed. This common personal bias has a widespread effect throughout the System. This common personal bias affects the judgment and actions of participants. For example, many new prosecutors would rather err on the side of protecting a child than allowing the child to be harmed. The attorney for the state may file an abuse and neglect petition every time CFS asks for one. If this occurs, the state's attorney will never have to live with the consequences of failing to intervene.

This may be good for the state's attorney, but as explained later in this guide, this "file every petition" position undermines the System when the cases are factually marginal. This problem and the reasoning behind it not only affects state's attorneys for the System but also the CPS as well.

A CPS, like a state's attorney, would rather err on the side of removing a child than allowing the child to remain with abusive parents. So here again, the CPS may draft supporting affidavits and ask state's attorneys to file petitions based on their affidavits on cases they know are marginal. Although this is safe, it too can negatively impact the System. A CPS, must use discretion and judgment when seeking to open a case in court.

Parents' attorneys, children's attorneys, GALs and other support providers who represent, protect and/or counsel parties in System cases all have to separate their desire to protect children from their professional judgment. Participants must do what the evidence dictates or the System will fail in the long run. For this reason, parties participating in the System must rely on the facts of the case and control their inner instinct to simply protect children. They must also be aware that not all care providers wear White Hats.

Many participants new to the System, including newly appointed judges, earnestly believe that those who work to protect children in the System are all there to do good. This "White Hat" philosophy, as referred to by those who have spent time practicing in the trenches, ignores the size of DPHHS and/or its CFS, the number of support providers within the System and the reality that people have different personalities. With the many people who are directly employed by CPS, or have contracted services with them, it's inevitable that there will be at least a few care providers who are not working to protect children but rather to fulfill their own personal interest.

The personal interest amongst some care providers will vary greatly from working for money to pay the rent to the far extreme of inflicting harm on children for personal gratification. Either way, System participants must remember that there is a chance that not everyone working a case is wearing a White Hat.

For example, *USA Today* published a story in 2013 titled: Cuffed boy found on porch with dead chicken around neck; parents jailed.[23] The story reported:

> A social services supervisor and a nurse face child abuse charges after an 11-year-old North Carolina boy was found handcuffed to a porch, shivering, with a dead chicken around his neck, Union County authorities say.
>
> Sheriff Eddie Cathey told USA TODAY the child was discovered Friday in frigid temperatures after neighbors complained about animals running loose at the home outside Monroe. Cathey said a deputy began interviewing Dorian Lee Harper, an emergency room nurse and the boy's foster parent, about the boy when another child opened the door and released several dogs that chased the deputy away.
>
> More deputies arrived and searched the home, finding five children, ages 14, 13, 11, 9 and 8. Harper and Wanda Sue Larson, both 57, had adopted four of the children and had been fostering the fifth, the child handcuffed to the porch, Cathey said.
>
> Larson is a supervisor with the Union County Department of Social Services. Cathey said his deputies had a good working relationship with Larson—and that both suspects were well-respected in their professions.
>
> "It's shocking to see how they lived," Cathey said. "The conditions were horrible. Trash, filth, animals and animal waste inside and outside the home. You could barely breathe inside that house." …
>
> "This investigation has only just begun," Cathey said. "We are fortunate that we were called. Sooner or later this situation could have ended in a child's death."

As this story illustrates, all five children were part of that community's system to protect children. The foster mother/adoptive mother of the children was a supervisor at the Department of Social Services in the community. The foster father/adoptive father of the children was employed as a professional

---

[23] John Bacon, *Boy Found with Dead Chicken around Neck; Parents Jailed*, USA TODAY, November 17, 2013.

nurse in the community. Both were highly regarded by the community and the court system. Many citizens must have thought these two people were there to protect their community's most vulnerable, young children who were previously removed from their abusive parents. Many wrongly concluded that this couple both wore White Hats.

This is just one example of how some people employed by or participating in the System as a care provider may put their personal interest over and above their duty to protect children. The naïve perception that all people working in the System are wearing white hats and are there to protect children threatens its neutrality. When this happens, children are not only harmed but the entire System and community suffers. Participants should be aware of this bias, since it not only contributes to imbalance, but may also contribute to a third System personal bias, the presumption of guilt.

Presumption of Guilt

Child abuse allegations are disturbing and unsettling and they often lead to a presumption that someone did harm the child. Many in the community may believe that a parent would not be accused of such a thing if the allegations were not true to some degree. Thus, the parent may go into the initial hearing with the burden of convincing the court, as well as the community, that he/she did not commit the alleged abuse.

Since parents are often perceived as guilty when charged (although "liable" is the legally correct word since System cases are civil), the parent and his or her attorney have a tough time proving they were not liable. Thus, parents may be found liable even in cases with marginal evidence. As one Montana attorney who specializes in civil litigation and occasionally accepts a court appointed System case once said, "A potted plant has a better chance of winning a show cause hearing than an experienced attorney!"[24] This attorney's statement sums up the effect the presumption of guilt bias can have on contested System hearings and how difficult it is for parents charged with abuse allegations to be found not liable at a contested hearing.

Personal Biases and Inherent Biases can both contribute to unbalancing a System. In addition to these two categories of biases, a third category exists, Avoidable Biases.

AVOIDABLE BIASES

Avoidable Biases are preventable prejudices that directly affect neutrality. When the System loses its neutrality, children, parents, extended family members and communities suffer. A good working system can become unbalanced by Avoidable Biases created by the organizations that appoint the attorneys to

---

[24] Jason Holden, Faure and Holden P.C., 2015.

represent the parents and children, the operating procedures of CFS, the way the GALs investigate their cases and report their findings back to the court, and the way prosecutors perform their System-related duties.

Petition Filing/Contract Attorneys

Attorneys representing the state in abuse and neglect cases must balance the interests of the victim, the victim's family, the alleged perpetrator and the perpetrator's family which is often part of the same family as the victim. They also have to balance the needs of CFS and the CPS. They have to consider the opinions of the many support providers, the attorneys, other court room participants and the public. As such, attorneys who represent the state must decide which cases to file.

Criminal prosecutors often have discretion as to whether to file or not file a felony charge. When they do, they use their judgment and experience to determine what charges to file as well as how to prosecute the case. An experienced prosecutor will only charge what can be proven. Experienced prosecutors do not let any one officer or witness dictate how the case is prosecuted. Although the prosecutor and officers might consult as a group, an experienced prosecutor will have the final say in whether the case will be prosecuted and how. An attorney for the state who is handling System cases must perform his/her duty in the same manner to help preserve the judicial docket and keep the System in balance.

One of the hardest parts of being an attorney for the state with System cases is screening the cases before filing to ensure that the court only hears cases that deserve judicial intervention. Some attorneys for the state file every abuse and neglect petition so they will never have to live with a child being hurt on their watch. This, "my client is the department and I will file every case they give me" philosophy to filing System cases does more harm than good. State's attorneys working for the System must use discretion in filing abuse and neglect court petitions similar to judgment used by criminal prosecutors in felony criminal cases.

System attorneys representing the states who fail to do this, risk creating an environment in which the courts become inundated with cases. Thus, to protect the court, the state's attorney must screen the cases. Backlog in the court's docket delays reunification of children with rehabilitated parents as well as the termination of parental rights when warranted. Such judicial delays slow the closing of cases. This adversely impacts how many new cases are investigated, opened and worked. In short, an unscreened flood of court filings undermines the entire System.

When an attorney for the state handling System cases decides not to file a petition in a given case, the attorney should contact the CPS who drafted the affidavit and explain to him/her why the case is not being filed. An experienced prosecutor will usually talk with the CPS about the different department safety tools and other organizations they could employ to continue monitoring the child's safety needs without having a formal judicial case opened. This way the System, with its many different federal and state programs and resources, can continue to work effectively without clogging the courts with cases.

This pertains to all attorneys for the state whether they work in-house or have been retained as a contract attorney. Contract attorneys, retained to represent the state or as more often done, represent parents and children, must understand System cases.

The United States Supreme Court requires states to ensure that a parent accused of abuse or neglect who is facing termination of parental rights is represented by an attorney. *Troxel v. Granville*, 530 U.S. 57, 65-66 (2000) The U.S. Supreme Court held, "[t]he liberty interest at issue in this case—the interest of parents in the care, custody, and control of their children—is perhaps the oldest of the fundamental liberty interests recognized by this Court." The Court further stated: "It is cardinal with us that the custody, care and nurture of the child reside first in the parents, whose primary function and freedom include preparation for obligations the state can neither supply nor hinder." *Id.* Thus, every state has a system in which attorneys are appointed by the courts or an agency to defend parents accused of child abuse. For this reason, and to avoid conflicts, contract attorneys often defend parents or represent the victim child.

In Massachusetts, for example, the Child and Family Law Division (CAFL) oversees all court-appointed child welfare attorneys.[25] This way, a majority of their dependency cases are handled by a panel of qualified private attorneys who are overseen by CAFL while staff attorneys handle the rest. New Jersey, on the other hand, has two separate programs within its public defender agency.[26] One program represents parents in child welfare cases while another program represents the children. Both New Jersey programs report to New Jersey's Chief Public Defender who oversees the programs.[27] In Montana, the Office of the State Public Defender (OPD) assigns a staff attorney to represent a parent, typically the custodial parent or offending parent, and then assigns the other parent to a contract attorney.[28]

In Systems that use contract attorneys to represent parents, it is often customary for the agency representing the accused to accept one of the parents as a client, and then contract out representation of the other parent. Typically the agency will represent the most offending parent while referring the other parent to a contract attorney. This not only reduces the chance of a conflict of interest

---

[25] The Public Defender Agency of Massachusetts, https://www.publiccounsel.net/hr/divisions.

[26] State of New Jersey's Office of the Public Defender, http://www.state.nj.us/defender/structure/olg.

[27] Proposal to create separate programs within the Agency, (2014), http://publicdefender.mt.gov/meetings/docs/03102014/DN-ParentRep.pdf.

[28] Proposal to create separate programs within the Agency, (2014), http://publicdefender.mt.gov/meetings/docs/03102014/DN-ParentRep.pdf.

occurring, it also helps ensure the parent with the most serious allegations gets an experienced System attorney.

Despite this safeguard, and to be sure the attorneys are qualified to work on System cases, all parties should be informed about the background and experience of the attorneys appointed to represent the state or defend the parents. Along these lines, one should also be aware of the background and experience of the Guardian Ad Litem (GAL) appointed to the case.

Guardian Ad Litem

A GAL is a special guardian appointed by the court to represent to the court what they believe to be in the child victim's best interest. The GAL's opinion may, depending on the age of the child, differ from the child's expressed wishes in certain cases. Thus, the role of a GAL can at times be very hard for the person performing this extremely important position.

A GAL may be an attorney or a caring community member. GALs may or may not receive compensation for their work. If paid, they may be paid by the court or an organization that solicits GALs. Whichever type of GAL is used, the GAL and the GAL program benefits the child if the GAL remains independent from the other parties.[29] Many judges rely heavily on the opinion and/or written report of the GAL. Some believe the GAL's written report to the court is the first document in the file the judge reads before hearing the case. For judges to rely on such a document, it is very important that it be written by a person who is independent of the System and remains independent in their duties with respect to the many different organizations that make up the System.[30]

Simply put, GAL programs must remain independent from CFS, the prosecutor, the parents' attorneys and the court. The individual GAL must remain independent of possible influences from care providers as well as other GALs representing other children in the case, even if the GAL stands alone.[31] If the GAL fails to remain independent of the offices, agencies, and personalities that make up their System, the GALs may contribute to their System losing its neutrality and becoming unbalanced.

A GAL or GAL office losing its independence is an Avoidable Bias that should be avoided by the volunteers, paid professionals, as well as the officers and board members who oversee the GAL program. Another area of the System that must remain independent of other System influences is the office that governs the CPS.

---

[29] *Independence Is What Judges Find Most Critical about the CASA Volunteer's Role,"* Judge Patricia A. Macias, 388th Judicial District, El Paso, TX, http://www.casaforchildren.org/site/c.mtJSJ7MPIsE/b.5926225/k.6569/What_Do_Judges_Think.htm.
[30] *Id.*
[31] *Id.*

Child Protection Specialist

A CPS may ultimately have the toughest job in the System. They have to investigate complaints, work with families informally, draft affidavits for court filings, testify in court hearings, care for children who are removed and help rehabilitate and/or educate parents with parenting skills. Along with these duties and tasks comes the emotional burden of protecting children. Dealing with the many different emotionally charged responsibilities and duties required of a CPS is a lot to ask of anyone on a daily basis. It is even more difficult if the CPS has not been properly trained and given continued support, or required to fill a quota requirement. Wrongly assuming that all CPS are equally competent is an Avoidable Biases that can be prevented.

To do the CPS job and process the feelings therefrom, a CPS needs to have the proper background, education, and initial training and then work in a supportive office environment. In many jurisdictions, the CPS must meet certain minimum State requirements and/or undergo required training before starting the position (or within a certain period after being hired).[32] This may not, however, be enforced in all jurisdictions or followed by CFS, especially when there is high CPS turnover or increased CPS hiring. Thus, one's perception about the CPS training may not reflect reality. The assumption of what is motivating the CPS may also be incorrect.

It has been rumored that some CFS agencies may impose a quota requirement to have a certain number of cases at all times.[33] Out of the open cases, some must be recently filed new cases, some heading towards reunification with other cases heading toward termination. Some professionals believe the quota requirement results from greed for federal money.

If a quota actually applies, it may be good for the agency's total yearly Federal financial assistance. It also can help administrators forecast individual department budgeting. It is not, however, good for the System, the community, the court system, or the children, parents, and family members in the System. By its very nature a quota necessarily ignores the reality that conditions change in a community from day to day.

A quota requirement forces the CPS to file cases they may not want to file, seek termination of parental rights in cases that may not warrant it, or reunify children with their parents before the parents are ready and able to parent. It disrupts the neutrality of the System in many ways, including how many cases are filed with the court. A quota requirement, if it is being implemented, is an undesirable Avoidable Bias that will contribute to the failure of a CFS office by undermining its objectives.

---

[32] Required Training, 110-1, *Montana's Child and Family Services Policy Manual* (2012).
[33] *Change Out of Tragedy?*, statement by four former employees of the regional CFSD, reported by Kristen Cates and Kimball Bennion, Great Falls Tribune, August 26, 2012.

When a CFS office fails, children are hurt. When children get hurt communities feeling the effects of a failed CFS speak out. Within time, if the state's CFS fails to regain its ability to protect children effectively, state legislatures will enact legislation to protect children and fix the CFS System. One such enactment is the appointment of an ombudsman to help oversee the System.

OMBUDSMAN

Often when communities within a state want to change a state-run program, the legislature will create an office to address complaints about that program. This office or position is frequently titled "the state's ombudsman." Although it may be titled differently, one common element exists, the position resulted from complaints about a governmental agency. This has occurred in over fifty percent of the states.[34] According to the National Conference of State Legislatures, 36 states have established a state or county office to assist in overseeing governmental actions including, but not limited to, their state's children's services. Out of those 36 states, 22 have established an office with duties and purposes specifically related to children's services. Of these, some have titled their overseeing office the Children's Ombudsman Office, while others have titled theirs the Office of the Child Advocate. Although the titles of the offices are different, their missions are similar: to address complaints about children's services.

The United States Ombudsman Association (USOA) defines the public sector ombudsman as "an independent, impartial public official with the authority and responsibility to receive, investigate or informally address complaints about government actions."[35] The USOA believes that an ombudsman must be impartial and independent of the department the ombudsman oversees. Unless the state's ombudsman is actually independent from the department it is overseeing, effective oversight is unlikely. Out of the 22 states referenced directly above, however, only eleven have established an office that is autonomous and independent of the office it is overseeing.[36]

Based on this set-up, many ombudsmen positions struggle to remain impartial and independent making the office less effective.[37] This, in turn, does more harm than good to a System that is failing to protect children. Failing to keep the ombudsman office independent from the organization it is overseeing will frustrate those who created the position and often proves unbeneficial to the State in the long run.

---

[34] Children's Ombudsman Offices/Office of the Child Advocate, (August 2012), http://www.ncsl.org/research/human-services/childrens-ombudsman-offices.aspx.

[35] Children's Ombudsman Offices / Office of the Child Advocate, Kate Bartell Nowak, (August 2012), www.ncsl.org/research/human-services/childrens-ombudsman-offices.aspx.

[36] Id.

[37] Alicia Caldwell, *New Colorado Child Protection Ombudsman Dennis Goodwin Talks about the Job Ahead*, Denver Post, December 14, 2013.

Thus, if your state has created such a position, investigate whether it is truly independent, impartial and able to make a change. Do not assume so just because the position was created. If not, help your legislature enact laws to ensure independence and give the ombudsman the power to investigate. Since an ombudsman rarely has the power to force System change, and because of the many different biases that exist and occur in the System, all parties must take control of the case and "drive the bus."

ALL PARTIES MUST DRIVE THE BUS

It is essential and extremely important that all parties, including the judge, ensure the case is being properly handled. All parties must ensure that the children at issue are safe, the parents' rights are being protected and keep the case moving forward either to reunification, guardianship, voluntary relinquishment or termination.

While addressing some of the issues being raised about the problem with the System in the state of Montana, the CFS administrator, Sarah Corbally, publicly stated in 2012: "It really is a larger system, we can't fix everything just from within."[38] She further said it was not just up to the department to make changes, there are many parties, including judges, involved in deciding what is best for kids and families. The words of Montana's CFS administrator makes it clear that all parties, including judges, must have an active role in keeping children safe and families strong.

To truly protect child victims, all parties must improve the effectiveness of the System by overseeing one another. Oversight guarantees that all parties are properly educated and trained in their respective roles to protect children and bring about parental change. In doing so, all resources within CFS, the community and the court should be used to investigate the issues and rehabilitate the parents while also protecting the children. If all parties "Drive the Bus" in System cases, they will ensure a case moves forward through the legal process and the proper outcome is achieved in a timely manner.

To accomplish this, all parties in the courtroom must be properly trained and work at ensuring that the case is being treated as a unique and individual case. They all must do what they can to not allow the many different biases discussed above to affect the result. Every court participant should demand that the right questions are asked during every hearing.

To gain further ideas on implementing a proactive program, and learn questions to ask and answers to seek at every stage of a case, one should understand the purpose of this Guide and how to accomplish its purposes.

---

[38] *Some Fear Agency's Lack of Reform*, Kristen Cates and Kimball Bennion, GREAT FALLS TRIBUNE, August 27, 2012.

PURPOSE OF THIS GUIDE

This Guide suggests minimum practice standards to help judges, parents' attorneys, children's attorneys, CFS workers, GALs and family members ask the questions that need to be asked in every case. It is paramount that participants do not leave these practice standards to those agencies or entities responsible for overseeing individual participants.

This Guide, if followed, should reduce costly formal court litigation by ensuring that all possible informal resources are implemented before a case is filed or shortly after TLC is granted. In either event, by using all the organizations and resources available within a community, there will be more transparency among the parties and a better chance of a successful reunification, timely guardianship, relinquishment or termination. Please use this Guide as what it is, a guide. Drive the bus, however, by custom tailoring what is done in your jurisdiction to give the parents, the child, the System and the courts the greatest possibility of success.

Introduction to the Sections

The Section part of this Guide breaks down and explains many different areas involved in a System case. Each Section may also include Help Aids that support the Section.

Sections begin with an introduction to the material and a statement of the issue. They then identify the participants and the duties each should perform. Each Section has a conclusion that is followed by a list of possible other issues that may need to be examined. This is followed by a timeline for performing required tasks and a narration explaining why the Section topic is important. Each Section contains feedback from individuals who read the book prior to final printing and may list possible bench cards that will assist the reader while practicing and/or participating in a System case. The Section may also include suggestions for other additional reading material.[39]

The authority cited in the footnotes of the Sections is from the United States Code, ABA published material or the Montana Code Annotated if not otherwise indicated. The cited Montana statutes reflect the current federal guidelines as of the date of printing, but one must consult each state's respective statutes and CFS policy manuals.

---

[39] The Checklists, Sample Forms and Bench Cards provided in this Guide are derived from many different sources including but not limited to the *ABA Child Safety Guide Bench Cards* and the *Montana Dependency and Neglect Best Practice Manual* (2013).

Receiving an Initial Report and Assigning a CPS

INTRODUCTION:

The Centralized Call Center (CCC) must determine the appropriate CFS response based on the type of initial report of abuse or neglect.

ISSUE:

Does the report warrant the assignment of a CPS to further investigate? If so, assign a qualified CPS who can respond in a timely manner.

PARTIES AND THEIR DUTIES:

1. CCC: Upon receiving a report, determine the appropriate level of response using guidelines based on state law, federal law, and the state's CFS policies. Some states use a tier system which categorizes the level of response that should be taken:[40]
2. CFS: When a CFS investigation is warranted, appoint a qualified CPS to respond to the report. CPS qualifications and on the job training differ from state to state but typically include requirements like: [41]
   - A college degree in social work or human services related field; and
   - Attendance at a twelve-week training program divided into:
     - Six weeks of classroom training; and
     - Six weeks in the field working with a supervisor.
3. CPS: Be prepared to explain (if the case proceeds to a formal contested court hearing), your background, education, experience, training and on-the-job mentoring received to date.

CONCLUSION:

Evaluating the report is important since CCC receives more calls on average than CFS has personnel to respond at any given time. Thus, CCC must screen the calls

---

[40] Montana's CFS Policy Manual (2013).
[41] Id.

properly, and CFS and CPS must understand the difference in response times according to their state's system.

If the court formally opens the case, the parties should factor the CPS qualifications and CFS experience into the weight of his/her testimony. If the investigating CPS lacks the minimum qualifications or training, the parties should request that a CPS supervisor assist with the case. Parties should inquire into the different areas during the initial court hearing to ensure that the CPS understands and can identify minimal standards required for parenting. It is also a good way for the court to get to know a little about the CPS who is practicing in front of the court.

OTHER ISSUES:

1. Should other governmental agencies be contacted to assist in the case?
2. Should other community-based organizations be contacted to assist in the case?

TIMELINE:

Check with your state for the respective deadlines in responding to abuse and neglect reports as well as fully investigate the reports.

WHY IMPORTANT:

Performing the above duties ensures that no report of abuse or neglect goes unanswered. It also informs the parties as to whether a qualified and properly trained CPS is assigned to the case.

FEEDBACK:

When courts inquire into the CFS response and investigation time, they can better understand how CFS operates. Asking the qualifications of CPS, especially the new faces in the courtroom, will show everyone that the court cares, which helps establish professionalism in the System. It also reinforces that CFS should assign qualified CPS to investigate a report or use supervisor support. Sending an unprepared CPS into the field is hard on the CPS, unfair to the family, and hurts the System in the long run.

HELP AID:

Checklist: Receiving a Report of Possible Abuse or Neglect

ADDITIONAL READING:

Child Safety, A Guide For Judges and Attorneys, Therese Lund and Jennifer Renne (2009).

CHECKLIST

Receiving a Report – Possible Abuse or Neglect

When an incident of abuse or neglect is reported, qualified personnel must determine the appropriate level of response and investigate the allegations. Ensuring the investigators' professional qualifications and timely response to the report helps all parties understand the reason for initial involvement as the case progresses in a professional manner.

QUESTIONS TO ANSWER

1. What type of report was received and what level of response did it get?
2. Was the response to the report within the state's statutory time period or in a timely manner?
3. Was the CPS who responded to the report properly educated, trained, and qualified to investigate the report?
4. If an inexperienced CPS investigated the report, was a supervisor consulted?

RED FLAGS

1. CPS is a newly hired person, at an office that is experiencing a high turnover rate, and has not had any supervisor assistance on the case.
2. The investigation occurred much later in time than when the incident was reported.

REPORT/INVESTIGATOR

1. Report investigated in a timely manner:

   O Yes

   O No, but the abuse re-occurred prompting intervention

   O No

2. The CPS was qualified to perform the initial investigation:

   O Yes

   O No, but consulted a supervisor before filing

   O No

Danger Assessment – To Remove or Not to Remove

INTRODUCTION:

The CPS assigned to investigate an initial report must determine whether the child's family can protect and care for the child in the current living conditions. CFS is encouraged to use recognized standards such as the family's history of CFS involvement, whether the incident is recurring or an isolated report, and face-to-face interviews with the victim, the parents, the complainant, any witnesses, relatives, and neighbors.

ISSUE:

Is the child safe or in danger, and if in danger, should the child be removed immediately from the child's current living conditions?

PARTIES AND THEIR DUTIES:

1. CPS:
   a. Investigate the factual allegations of the report by performing a Danger Assessment for the child and determine whether the factual allegations of abuse or neglect are unfounded (not true), unsubstantiated (not sure), or substantiated (validated as true);
   b. If the allegations are substantiated, determine whether further investigation is required or if CFS intervention should be initiated;
   c. If the allegations are substantiated, determine whether the child must be removed or if the danger can be removed;
   d. If the child is removed, place the child in the least traumatizing environment as possible, typically identified in order of priority by state statute; and
   e. Be prepared to explain the findings of the Danger Assessment to the court.
2. CPS Supervisor:
   a. Consult with the CPS and ensure that the assessment complied with the policy of the state's CFS; and

b. Assist in uploading/posting the assessment on the state's child welfare information system.

CONCLUSION:

It is important for a CPS to perform the Danger Assessment properly since it is used to determine whether the child is safe. If the child is not safe, it helps determine whether the child should be removed from his or her environment. If the CPS is new, the worker should seek guidance from a supervisor, since no child should remain in an abusive environment or be unnecessarily removed.

OTHER ISSUES:

If the child is an Indian child as defined by the Indian Child Welfare Act (ICWA), see the additional requirements, which must be satisfied before removal and the statutory priorities for child placement.

TIMELINE:

1. The CPS should consult with his or her supervisor within 24 hours of the first face-to-face contact with all children in the family.
2. If the child has not been placed with a relative, a family identification meeting should be held with known family members within 30 days of removal to locate a suitable family placement.

WHY IMPORTANT:

Performing a Danger Assessment helps verify that the initial report is legitimate and that the child is not temporarily removed from the custodial parents without reason, or worse, left to remain in an abusive setting. It is also important to identify whether the parents will be cooperative and, if utilizing an in-home safety agreement, will protect the child while the parents receive services.

FEEDBACK:

By reviewing CFS Danger Assessment, all parties will know from the onset of the case whether CFS implemented the least intrusive approach to keep the child safe and to remedy the threat of danger. It documents what CFS has done in the case to-date. This way all parties can determine whether CFS correctly evaluated whether the child was safe, whether CFS initiated proper services to control the threats of danger, and whether CFS made reasonable efforts to avoid removal of the child. A group approach is recommended when possible.

HELP AID:

Checklist: Danger Assessment – To Remove or Not to Remove

ADDITIONAL READING:

Your state's CFS Present Danger Assessment form

CHECKLIST

Danger Assessment – To Remove or Not to Remove

Complete a Danger Assessment to determine whether the reported allegations of abuse or neglect are unfounded, unsubstantiated or substantiated and if danger exists, whether the child should be removed from his/her home or if an in-home safety plan is sufficient to control the danger and keep the child safe. A threat of danger can be created by a lack of ability or capacity of a family member, a specific family situation or a personal behavior created by a preconceived perception or motive. The CPS should be able to answer the areas of required information listed below by conducting interviews with the child, parents, complainant, witnesses, or relatives and neighbors.

QUESTIONS TO ANSWER

1. What type of abuse or neglect or substantial risk was occurring?
2. How severe was the abuse or neglect and what were the resulting injuries?
3. Who resides at the child's home: one parent, both parents, siblings, family, and/or roommates?
4. Who is the party most responsible for the threat of danger: mother, father, step-parent, or other?
5. Does the person threatening the danger have a history of violence or threatening behavior and can he/she control their behavior, or is it impulsive?
6. Does alcohol or substance abuse trigger the threat of danger?
7. Is the threat triggered by a specific event such as when bills are due or pay is received?
8. Is the threat triggered by a physical condition of the parent, like back pain or a migraine headache?
9. Is there a pattern to the threats, like daily or weekly, or is the threat of danger unpredictable?
10. How long have the threats of danger been occurring? Is it an isolated incident or a recurring pattern of abuse?
11. How do the parents perceive the child?
12. Is the child truly loved and if so, by whom?
13. Does one or both parents have sufficient parenting knowledge and skill to take care of the child?

14. Which parent is routinely in the home performing the essential child-raising duties?

15. Are the parents' protective capacities sufficient to protect the child when threats emerge?

16. Are the parents willing to cooperate with CFS and voluntarily consent to a safety agreement and if so, would the family be able to follow and abide by a safety agreement?

17. If a safety agreement is initiated, how many services are required, how often would the assistance be needed, and how long would the agreement need to be in effect?

18. Is the parent motivated to care for the child and assure that his/her basic needs are met?

19. Is the household situation predictable enough that if CFS' informal safety agreement and community programs are put in place, the threat of danger will be managed or eliminated?

20. If the family objects to CFS intervention, what is the main reason for rejecting the help?

21. What is the child's mental and physical health as well as his/her physical capacity?

22. Does the child have any unmet needs: emotional, physical, or educational?

23. Does the family have sufficient resources to provide the child with food and shelter and other basic needs?

24. Does the child's home meet minimal standards or does it endanger the child's physical health?

25. Has the child been reported in poor physical condition in the past and if yes, when?

26. Has the child been reported as neglected and if so, how?

27. Has the child received any serious unexplained or suspicious physical injuries?

28. Has the child disclosed sexual abuse?

29. Is the child afraid and if yes, of whom or what?

RED FLAGS

1. Child has suffered an injury at the hands of a parent.

2. Child shows symptoms of emotional trauma which should be immediately addressed.

3. Child lacks behavioral control or is exhibiting self-destructive behavior and the parent is not responding appropriately.

4. The parent(s) previously failed to follow a reasonable safety agreement and/or have extensive CFS history.

5. One or more of the family members residing in the residence are known to be violent or dangerous.

REMOVE OR NOT TO REMOVE

1. **No Danger:** The child is safe, no immediate threat exists and/or the family has protective capacities sufficient to protect the child.
   - O Child is safe and no immediate threats exist – No removal:
     - O Close case (no follow-up required);
     - or -
     - O Case remains open with a Voluntary Safety Agreement in place.
2. **Present Danger:** Child has been harmed and/or is in an unsafe environment:
   - O CFS keeps the case open and:
     - O No removal – the danger has been controlled and a safety plan is in place;
     - or -
     - O Child is removed and placed in an out of the home setting; and
       - O CPS drafts an affidavit in a timely manner and delivers it to the state's attorney so a petition can be filed with the court.
3. **Impending Danger:** Harm may occur to the child in the present situation.
   - O No removal – the case remains open with a Voluntary Safety Agreement in place;
     -or-
   - O CFS files a petition with the court, and:
     - O No removal – the danger has been remedied and a safety agreement is in place;
     - or -
     - O Child is removed and placed elsewhere following state and Federal legal standards.
4. **Child Maltreatment:** Child has suffered from abuse or neglect which is either recurring or is specific to an isolated incident or event.
   - O Same action as 3) above
5. **Child Fatality:** A child has died as a result of abuse or neglect.
   - O Is there another child that is at risk?
     - O If yes, follow 3) above;
     - and -
     - O If no, close CFS case and assist state criminal prosecutors with their investigation.

CPS Supervisor Assessment:

O CPS supervisor reviewed completed Danger Assessment; and

O Upon approval, assessment was uploaded and saved in CFS computer tracking system.

Comprehensive Family Functioning Assessment

INTRODUCTION:

After the initial Danger Assessment, and if the case remains open, CFS comprehensively assesses both the child and the family. This investigation should examine the child's vulnerabilities and the protective capacities of the parents. It should also include a comprehensive examination into the parent's feelings toward the child and their desire and ability to function as a parent.

ISSUE:

Is this a vulnerable child and can the child's parents or caregivers function with the minimum ability required to safely raise the child?

PARTIES AND THEIR DUTIES:

1. CPS:
   a. Evaluate the child's and parents' cognitive, behavioral, and emotional abilities;
   b. Evaluate both parents' actions, the parents' family functioning, and their ability to provide for the child; and
   c. Determine whether the child can be protected and/or the family can function with an in-home safety agreement, or should the child be removed.

CONCLUSION:

CFS should determine how best to proceed in the case, either informally with a CFS safety plan in place, possibly assisted by other community organizations, or formal court intervention.

OTHER ISSUES:

1. Complete the Family Functioning Assessment and give it to the state's attorney.

2. The state's attorney should file the Family Functioning Assessment as a supplemental report with the court.

TIMELINE:

CFS will require completion of a comprehensive family functioning assessment within a certain number of days of removal but the timeframe is state-specific.

WHY IMPORTANT:

A Family Functioning Assessment helps ensure the family received a comprehensive, fair, and unbiased investigation into the allegations against them. Performing the assessment early in the case, when possible, will help all parties understand the possibility of reunification under a safety plan or if a petition for TIA or TLC needs to be filed. Similarly, performing the assessment early will give the CPS a heightened insight as to the expected cooperation level of the parties as well as the amount of CFS assistance, if any, which will be required.

FEEDBACK:

Do not expect every party to participate voluntarily in the assessment early in the case. Many parents will not cooperate in the evaluation until they are court ordered to do so.

HELP AIDS:

Checklist: Child Safety Assessment
Checklist: Family/Parenting Functioning Assessment

ADDITIONAL READING:

Your state's CFS Child Safety Assessment and a Family Functioning Assessment forms.

CHECKLIST

Child Safety Assessment

Thoroughly assess the child's vulnerabilities and whether the child has self-protecting ability to determine whether an in-home safety agreement is sufficient to control the danger and keep the child safe. The parties should be able to provide the required information listed below from the information the CPS obtained during the initial interviews with the child, parents, complainant, witnesses, relatives, and neighbors and all subsequent interviews and additional reports.

QUESTIONS TO ANSWER

1. How old is the child (0-3/4-5) or (6-11/12-18)?
2. Can the child communicate effectively about his/her situation?
3. Does the child feel safe and secure with one or both of his/her parents?
4. Does the child fear remaining in the home, and if yes, why?
5. What is the child's size and mobility and does he/she have any physical disabilities?
6. What is the child's emotional state and does he/she have any intellectual or developmental disabilities?
7. Does the child have any behavioral or temperament problems?
8. What is the child's educational level and skill?
9. How is the child doing in school and what are his/her relationships with teachers and other students?
10. How is the child's personal development and intellect?
11. Can the child anticipate and judge the presence of danger?
12. Will the child recognize that a dangerous situation is developing or recognize it once it is happening?
13. Can the child articulate and report danger?
14. What is the child's social development and peer relations?
15. Does the child have good friends?
16. Are there other issues that would prevent the child from self-protecting?
17. Does the child consciously know what provokes or stimulates the threat of danger to him/her?

18. Does the child behave and respond in a way that escalates the threat of danger to the child?

19. Has the child demonstrated self-protection by properly responding to previous threats?

20. Does the child have a plan to protect himself/herself if the threat of danger arises?

21. Besides defending himself/herself from threats, can the child care for his/her own basic needs?

22. Are there siblings living in the home, and if so, do they need to be protected and can they help protect the child at issue?

23. Is the child isolated from his/her community (rural living/home schooling/no close family)?

RED FLAGS

1. Child has been previously unsuccessful in self-protecting himself/herself.

2. Child remains physically, mentally, or emotionally fragile from a prior parental maltreatment.

SAFETY AGREEMENT (IN-HOME) VS REMOVAL

1. **Vulnerabilities:**

   O Yes, the child has vulnerabilities that may cause a threat of danger to the child;

   - or -

   O Yes, the child has vulnerabilities, but they do not currently cause a threat of danger to the child;

   - or -

   O No, the child has no vulnerabilities that pose a threat of danger to the child.

2. **Ability to Self-Protect:**

   O No, the child lacks the ability to self-protect;

   - or -

   O Yes, the child does have the ability to self-protect.

CPS Supervisor Assessment:

   O CPS supervisor reviewed completed Child Safety Assessment;
   - and -

   O Upon approval, assessment was uploaded and saved in CFS child welfare information system.

CHECKLIST

Parenting Assessment and Family Functioning

Thoroughly assess the parents and/or parents' parental actions and their ability to parent to further determine whether an in-home safety agreement is sufficient to control the danger and keep the child safe. The CPS should be able to provide the required information below from the information CFS obtained during their initial interviews with the child, parents, complainant, witnesses, relatives, neighbors, and any subsequent interviews and additional reports.

QUESTIONS TO ANSWER

A. **Evaluate the Offending Parent's Actions:**

1. Can the parent adequately explain the event that triggered the investigation?
2. Has the parent threatened serious physical harm to the child?
3. Has the parent threatened others and if so, was it in front of the child?
4. Is there a feeling of attachment between the parent and child?
5. Does the parent blame the child for the CFS and/or the court's involvement?

B. **Evaluate the Non-Offending Parent's Actions:**

1. Has the parent demonstrated the ability to protect the child or others in the past?
2. Has the parent expressed his/her intention to prevent this incident from reoccurring?
3. Does the parent display concern for the child having to experience the abuse or neglect?
4. Does the parent believe an incident took place that affected the child's safety?
5. Has the parent clearly demonstrated that the safety and well-being of the child is a priority?
6. Is the parent free from problems which might affect the child's safety such as severe depression, lack of impulse control, or medical needs?
7. Does the parent demonstrate the ability to correct problems and adapt to new challenges?
8. What was the parent's reaction to CPS intervention?

C. **Evaluate the Parent's Functioning:** (of the primary parent raising the child or both parents if they are together in a relationship or parenting jointly)

1. Does the parent have the general knowledge to care for the child?
2. Does the parent understand the child's needs (emotional/physical/developmental)?
3. What is the parent's perception of what a parent does or should do?
4. Does the parent want to be a parent and do they get any satisfaction from being a parent?
5. What level of intellect, problem solving, and communication skills does the parent possess?
6. How does the parent cope with his/her own stress and problems as they arise?
7. What is the current employment and employment history of the parents?
8. Did the parent refuse CPS access to the child?
9. Does CPS believe the parents will flee?
10. What is the criminal history of the parents?
11. Does the parent have issues with substance abuse and has he/she been in treatment?
12. Does the parent understand the different stages of child development?
13. Does the parent understand age appropriate discipline and the purpose thereof?
14. Does the parent utilize routines and boundaries?
15. Does the parent exhibit consistency in parenting among all their children?
16. Is the parent's expectation of the child realistic?
17. Is the parent influenced by other family members and/or friends and if so, is this a positive influence?
18. Does the parent understand that he/she is responsible for the care and protection of the child?
19. Does the parent have the ability to recognize signs indicating that danger is pending?
20. Will the parent act appropriately when he/she recognizes the child is in danger or danger is pending?
21. Is the parent intellectually and emotionally able to protect the child and if so, is that his/her intent?
22. Does the parent have the emotional strength and/or energy to raise a child?
23. Is the parent realistic in his/her cognitive thought processes in that they perceive reality accurately?
24. Are there any cultural practices that may be an issue?

D. **Evaluate the Parent's Ability to Provide for Child:** (of the primary parent raising the child or both parents if they are together in a relationship or parenting jointly)

1. Is the parent physically able to protect the child and if so, does he/she intend to do so?
2. Is the parent independent?
3. Does he/she have the decision making ability to maintain a home?
4. Does the parent use the resources available to meet the child's basic needs?
5. Does the child have bedroom furniture (bed/bedding/alarm clock)?
6. Does the child have clothes to wear, food to eat, and personal hygiene items?
7. Will the parent ensure the child maintains good hygiene, receives breakfast, lunch and dinner?
8. Can the parent wake the child up for school, ensure the child attends school, and help with school work and obtaining school supplies?
9. Does the family have a vehicle and an approved car seat?
10. Will the parents ensure the child is transported to doctor appointments, dentist appointments, eye exams, and after school programs and/or sports activities?
11. Is the parent able to meet his/her emotional needs as well as help the child when the child becomes emotional?
12. Does the parent have adequate knowledge and skill to perform responsible parenting tasks?

RED FLAGS

1. Parents do not have a permanent place of residence (i.e., an apartment/mobile home/house).
2. Parents do not have any means of transportation.
3. Parents expresses more concern for paramour than for child.
4. Parents are suffering from substance abuse.

SAFETY PLAN (IN-HOME) VS REMOVAL

1. **Parental Actions:**
   - O May pose a threat of danger to the child;
   - O Are questionable but do not pose a threat of danger to the child; or
   - O Are normal in light of the circumstances.

     - and -

2. **Ability to Parent:**
   - O Parent lacks the ability to parent the child to minimal standards; or
   - O Parent has the ability to parent the child properly.
     - and -

3. **Ability to Provide:**
   - O Parent lacks the ability to provide for the child to minimal standards; or
   - O Parent has the ability to provide for the child properly.

CPS Supervisor Assessment:
   - O CPS supervisor reviewed completed Family Functioning Safety Assessment;
     - and -
   - O Upon approval, assessment was uploaded and saved in CFS child welfare information system.

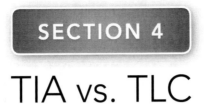

SECTION 4

TIA vs. TLC

INTRODUCTION:

Some states offer two types of remedies, Temporary Investigative Authority (TIA) is a grant of authority from the court authorizing CFS to conduct an investigation into allegations of child abuse, neglect, or abandonment. TIA typically only lasts for 90 days. Temporary Legal Custody (TLC), on the other hand, gives CFS custody and responsibility of the child, according to law, for up to six months.

ISSUE:

If your State offers two types of remedies, TIA or TLC, should the case be filed as a TIA case which will give CFS additional time to complete a full investigation before determining whether to move for adjudication, or ask directly for TLC which requires adjudication by a court?

PARTIES AND THEIR DUTIES:

1. CPS Supervisor: Orally approve the CPS petition for TLC.
2. State's attorney:
   a. Consult with the CPS, review the facts known to-date and determine whether the State can legally meet the required standard of proof for the court to order TLC;
   b. If yes to "a." above, and the case warrants a formal judicial proceeding, draft, file and circulate a petition for TLC; or
   c. If no to "a." above, draft a petition for TIA and an investigation itinerary detailing what CFS request to investigate and an expected completion timeline.

CONCLUSION:

TIA is a useful procedural tool to entice cooperation by the parties, maintain the unity of the family, and reduce litigation.[42] In some cases parents are less threatened by TIA than TLC, which may increase their cooperation. In other cases, TIA provides the parents an opportunity to show that they can protect

---

[42] *Montana Dependency and Neglect Best Practice Manual* (2013).

and provide for their child without formal intervention. In all cases, however, the decision to file a petition for TIA should be discussed and made jointly with a supervisor.

TIA can, unfortunately, also be used by CFS as a tool against the parents to get cases opened judicially when there are little or no facts of abuse or neglect reported or identified. When this occurs, it undermines the spirit of TIA and the parties' belief in TIA. Another misuse of TIA is when CFS knows from the onset of the case that TLC will be required but initially asks only for TIA.

To prevent TIA misuse, the court should inquire if a voluntary safety agreement was proposed, and if not, why. The court should also inquire into the specific areas of investigation and set a realistic deadline for the investigation to be completed.

OTHER ISSUES:

1. When TIA is sought, the court only conducts a show cause hearing.
2. A grant of TIA allows CFS to make decisions regarding the child's care and placement, and the state should include a request for emergency protective services in their TIA petition.
3. When moving for TLC, a show cause hearing and an adjudication hearing should be scheduled. In contested cases, the hearings should be bifurcated to avoid confusion with the different rules of evidence that apply to the hearings.

TIMELINE:

CPS should determine whether to file for TIA or TLC within two days of removal of the child from the parents.

WHY IMPORTANT:

TIA, when done properly, can give CFS a better working relationship with the parents and may help CFS determine that a case should be dismissed with a safety plan in place. This is beneficial since a good working relationship between CFS and the parents can help throughout the case. In some cases, the resulting foundation of trust and cooperation gives those parents a greater chance of rehabilitation and reunification. Additionally, when TIA is initiated for the right reasons, it may expedite the TLC process and/or reunification if TLC subsequently becomes necessary.[43] TIA should be used properly and monitored by all parties, since it allows the parents to avoid the possibility of the negative consequences of an adjudication, which is good but can also be misused.

---

[43] Montana Dependency and Neglect Best Practice Manual (2013).

FEEDBACK:

TIA is an important procedural tool for CFS. It should be used in cases that warrant additional investigation. It should not, however, be used to avoid conflict during the hearing where CFS knows the situation really requires TLC. To prevent any possible abuse of TIA, a court should ensure that an investigation plan with objective areas of investigation is in place. All parties should do what they can to not allow TIA to simply become an invitation for CPS to begin an inquisition.

HELP AID:

Checklist: TIA vs TLC – Advantages and Disadvantages

CHECKLIST

TIA vs TLC – Advantages and Disadvantages

Whether a child and his/her family will be better served via TIA rather than TLC is an important question for the parties to determine. TIA, when appropriate, can have several advantages over TLC.

TIA ADVANTAGES:

1. May help to maintain family unity;
2. Encourages cooperation among the parties;
3. Reduces litigation and saves judicial resources;
4. Provides the parents an opportunity to prove to CFS that they can safely parent their child; and
5. Avoids negative consequences from being adjudicated as an abusive or neglectful parent.

POTENTIAL DISADVANTAGES:

CFS may find more factual evidence of parental abuse or neglect later when TLC is sought.

QUESTIONS TO ANSWER

1. Was a voluntary safety agreement proposed to the parents, and if not, why not?
2. What specific issues of concern does CFS want to further investigate?
3. Does CFS have a timeframe for the investigation?

RED FLAGS

1. TIA is being sought rather than TLC in a case where the evidence clearly establishes a pattern of abuse or neglect.
2. TIA is being sought with no areas of further factual investigation identified.

TIA VS TLC

Voluntary Safety Agreement is not an adequate means of ensuring child safety and/or parental assistance, even with the many different community care services available.

1. **TIA:**
   - O Specific issues of abuse or neglect have been identified and need additional investigation.
   - O The time period for said investigation has been conveyed and appears reasonable.
2. **TLC:** Harm may occur to the child in the present situation.
   - O TIA is not warranted and TLC must be sought by the state to protect the child and/or rehabilitate the parents.

SECTION 5

Drafting an Affidavit in Support of a Court Petition

INTRODUCTION:

The CPS must draft an affidavit stating the specific facts to justify the court granting emergency protective services pending a show cause hearing.

ISSUE:

Do the relevant facts establish probable cause to believe that the child was at imminent risk of harm? The affidavit should also establish that the action taken by CFS was reasonably necessary to avert future harm.[44]

PARTIES AND THEIR DUTIES:

1. CPS: Draft an accurate, concise and factually specific affidavit establishing the issues above and attach supporting material like medical treatment records, school or childcare testimony, parent interviews, interviews of siblings and/or proof of previous involuntary removals. The affidavit should also include clear, specific and objective reasons why a Voluntary Safety Agreement is not feasible.[45]
2. CPS Supervisor: Review the CFS affidavit and if approved ensure it is delivered to the state's prosecuting attorney in a timely manner.
3. State's Prosecuting Attorney: Confer with CPS to ensure the affidavit contains sufficient facts for filing and if not, discuss the possibility of an alternative informal method of providing services and safety.

CONCLUSION:

CPS must evaluate the facts of the case and determine whether the alleged danger, if true, can be remedied via community care provider assistance programs and/or a CPS voluntary services agreement. If true, try to work with

[44] *Mueller v. Auker*, 576 F.3d 979, 991-992 (9th Cir. Idaho 2009); *see also Springer v. Placer County*, 338 Fed. Appx. 587, 590 (9th Cir. Cal. 2009).
[45] *Montana Dependency and Neglect Best Practice Manual* (2013).

the family on a voluntary basis and develop an appropriate plan that protects the child and remedies the danger. If a voluntary services agreement will not be sufficient, draft a factually accurate affidavit to give to the state's attorney.

OTHER ISSUES:

CPS should attach their document that details the findings of the Present Danger Assessment, the Child Safety Assessment and the Family Functioning Assessment to the affidavit to ensure that all parties know of the findings.

TIMELINE:

If CPS removes a child from his/her parents, the CPS should submit an affidavit to the attorney for the state within the time frame set by the state.

WHY IMPORTANT:

All parties are judged by their professionalism from the beginning of a case and a CPS' reputation rests in part on the affidavit he/she submits. Thus, an accurate affidavit with supporting evidence attached is key to establishing how thoroughly and professionally the CPS will act while working the case.

FEEDBACK:

The CPS may not have the information and/or time to draft a concise and factually detailed affidavit in some cases.

HELP AID:

Checklist: CPS Affidavit in Support of a Court Petition

CHECKLIST

CPS Affidavit in Support of a Court Petition

The affidavit in support of a petition for court intervention is where every formal case begins and therefore should be well written. A boiler plate, non-specific affidavit, sets the stage for sloppy work and an unprofessional image. Thus, a CPS should always remember others review the document and question any incomplete information or inadequate explanation.

QUESTIONS TO ANSWER

1. Was a voluntary services agreement proposed to the parent, and if not, why not?
2. Does the affidavit set forth the details of the alleged abuse and neglect?
3. Did the affidavit include supporting evidentiary attachments, and if not, why not?
4. Was the affidavit reviewed by a supervisor, and if not, why not?

RED FLAGS

1. Affidavit is short on facts and heavy on speculation.

AFFIDAVIT IN SUPPORT OF A COURT PETITION

O Voluntary Services Agreement is not an adequate means of child safety and/or parental assistance, not even with the many different community care services available.

1. **CPS Believes Probable Cause Exists, in that:**
   O Child is at imminent risk of harm;
   - and -
   O CFS action was reasonably necessary to avert future harm.

2. **Factual Details:**
   O Stated accurately and concisely.

3. **Supporting Evidence:**
   O Medical treatment records;
   O School or childcare testimony;
   O Interviews of parents, victim, siblings of victim;
   - and -
   O DPHHS family history.

4. **CFS Attachments:**
   - O Voluntary Services Agreement;
   - O Danger Assessment;
   - O Child Safety Assessment;
     - and/or-
   - O Family Functioning Assessment

Drafting and Filing a Petition with the Court

INTRODUCTION:

The state's attorney must determine whether the state can prove the facts stated in the CPS affidavit, and if the facts are proven true, whether they justify the court granting emergency protective services. If yes, draft and file a petition with the court seeking either TIA or TLC (adhering to the original intent of each).

ISSUE:

Do the facts that can be proven show the child is at imminent risk of harm and the action taken by CFS is reasonably necessary to avert future injury?

PARTIES AND THEIR DUTIES:

1. State's Attorney:
   a. Examine the facts for litigation purposes and review the legal standard to be proven at the show cause hearing;
   b. Draft and file a petition for either TIA or TLC and accompanying order with the court granting CFS emergency protective services over the child as well as the relief sought in the CPS affidavit; and
   c. Meet with the witnesses and interview them before the hearing.
2. CPS:
   a. Provide the state's attorney with a copy of any safety plans or voluntary services agreements or articulate why a plan was not possible; and
   b. If the child was removed, identify in writing what must occur before reunification.
3. CPS supervisor: Help the CPS prepare to testify in the courtroom.

CONCLUSION:

The state's attorney must evaluate the CPS affidavit and determine whether the alleged facts, if proven true, meet the required level of proof by law. If yes, the attorney should consult with the CPS and his/her supervisor and then prepare a petition and file it with the court. If the facts of the case do not meet the legal standard, advise the CPS of the reasons why a petition will not be prepared and suggest alternative actions by which CFS could informally monitor the safety of the child.

OTHER ISSUES:

1. When filing a petition, the state's attorney should ensure that the state's discovery file is ready to be shared with all parties as soon as the court accepts the case since procedural time periods in System cases are often shortened.
2. Service of process is important since strict legal compliance is required. Non-compliance can cause delay or dismissal.
3. CPS should work with the family, if they are willing to stipulate to the issues of concern and accept assistance, to begin rehabilitation efforts and services.

TIMELINE:

The state's attorney should file a petition with the court within the timeframe set by their state's statutes after receiving the affidavit from the CPS.

WHY IMPORTANT:

The state's attorney is the gate keeper between CFS and the court system. The prosecutor should treat a CFS affidavit similar to law enforcement information in criminal felony cases and exercise prosecutorial discretion before filing.

FEEDBACK:

It helps when the state's attorney works in conjunction with the CPS to agree collaboratively on which legal remedy is appropriate for the specific case. A collective approach is more efficient and typically yields better end results.

HELP AID:

Checklist: State's Petition for Court Intervention

ADDITIONAL READING:

Making Sense of ASFA Regulations, A Roadmap for Effective Implementation, by Debra Ratterman Baker (Editor), Diane Boyd Rauber (Editor), ABA Center on Children and the Law (Corporate Author), http://www.americanbar.org.

CHECKLIST

State's Petition for Court Intervention

The state's petition asking the court for judicial intervention should explain why emergency protective services are required. The petition is the first pleading in the case file. The state's attorney should ensure it meets the four-corner test of legality.

QUESTIONS TO ANSWER

1. After reviewing the CPS affidavit, does the state's attorney agree that the situation warrants the filing of a petition, and if not, why not?
2. Does the state's attorney agree with the relief being sought (TIA or TLC), and if not, why not?

RED FLAGS

1. A boiler plate affidavit containing factual errors was submitted by the CPS.
2. The CPS has little experience in evaluating cases and was not assisted by a supervisor.

STATE'S PETITION FOR COURT INTERVENTION

1. **Petition:**
   - O Contains accurate and concise factual details of abuse or neglect with supporting evidence and/or appropriate CFS investigation documents;
     - and-
   - O Probable cause exists to believe the child is at imminent risk of harm and CFS action was reasonably necessary to avert future harm.

2. **Services of Process:**
   - O Petition was properly served on all known parties as required by law.

Show Cause Hearing

INTRODUCTION:

The court must determine whether the state has proved the facts in its petition and whether those facts are sufficient for continued court intervention. The court must also decide whether the child should be removed from his/her place of residence and if already removed, whether the child should remain removed or be returned home immediately.

ISSUE:

Do the proven facts meet the required legal standard to grant CFS the power of emergency protective services over the child and if so, did CFS make reasonable efforts to avoid removing child from his/her home?

PARTIES AND THEIR DUTIES:

1. Court: (primary goal is to ensure that the child will be safe)
   a. Inform the parties that the purpose of the proceeding is to ensure the safety of the child while preserving the unity and welfare of the family whenever possible;[46]
   b. Determine whether:
      i. The allegations of the petition were proven or admitted, and if so, does probable cause exist for continued CFS protective services intervention; and
      ii. CFS made reasonable efforts to avoid removing the child and placing him/her in a protective placement;
   c. If CFS intervention is continued, decide whether the child can be returned home safely at the current time by evaluating:
      i. Whether threats of danger exist within the family;
      ii. If threats exist, whether the child is vulnerable to such threats; and
      iii. Whether the parents have sufficient protective capacities to manage or control said threats.[47]

---

[46] 45 CFR § 1356.21(b).
[47] *Child Safety Guide for Judges and Attorneys*, American Bar Association (2009).

    d. Issue an order in a timely manner, and if removal occurs or continues, ensure that the child is placed in accordance with priority placements if plausible, while trying to protect the child's right to a healthy and safe childhood in a potentially permanent placement.

2. State: Present evidence to warrant the court granting emergency protective services TIA to CFS.

3. Attorneys: Represent their clients as required by law following their state's ethical standards as well as state and federal statutory guidance.

CONCLUSION:

The court should conduct a thorough hearing and make an informed decision as to whether or not to uphold a child's removal by CFS. The longer a child is removed, the more the bond between the child and his/her parents is disrupted. On the contrary, the longer the child is left in an abusive environment, the more harm the child will suffer. The child, the parents and all other parties deserve a properly conducted hearing.

OTHER ISSUES:

1. Rules of Evidence apply but child hearsay is allowed.
2. Inquire into whether the child is an Indian child under the ICWA and if so, verify compliance with ICWA.[48]
3. Ensure any GAL appointed has been properly trained and possesses the proper experience for the case. The order appointing said GAL should explain the role, expected duties and GAL's authority.
4. Stipulations to emergency protective services and TIA or TLC over the child are usually allowed. Also, the parties may stipulate to the child's out of home placement pending the dispositional hearing.
5. If the parents admit the allegations, CFS should draft an appropriate treatment plan or an investigation plan and circulate it to the parties ten days before the next scheduled hearing so the parents can began working on it.
6. The Court's order must indicate that CFS made "reasonable efforts" to prevent removal of the child, or CFS may be permanently disqualified from receiving federal funds for foster care throughout the life of the case.[49]
7. Court Ordered Mediation (see the following section on Mediation).

TIMELINE:

1. Show Cause Hearing should be scheduled within 20 days from the date on which the initial petition was filed, except as provided under ICWA.

---

[48] The case is subject to ICWA if it involves an Indian child, defined as a child who either is enrolled in a federally recognized Indian tribe or is eligible for enrollment and is the biological child of a member of an Indian tribe. 25 USC § 1903(4).

[49] 45 CFR §§ 1356.21(b)(1)(ii) and (d)(2).

2. Adjudication is allowed during the Show Cause Hearing but is discouraged if the Show Cause Hearing is contested. (see Section 9, Adjudication Hearing for reasoning.)

WHY IMPORTANT:

The show cause hearing is important since it allows the parties to dispute the facts stated in the CPS affidavit and thereby disprove that the child was in imminent risk of harm at the time of removal. It also gives the parties an opportunity to stipulate to the issues of danger, so treatment and reunification can occur faster. The parties also can further challenge whether CFS' actions were reasonably necessary to avert the specified injury.[50]

FEEDBACK:

Some state statutes allow for a combined show cause and adjudication hearing. Some experienced practitioners believe the two hearings should be combined only if the parties are not contesting the issues and the parents are stipulating to the court granting TIA or TLC. Others believe that in contested cases the court should bifurcate the two hearings and hold them separately to avoid confusion about which standard of proof and which rules of evidence apply.

HELP AID:

Bench Card: Show Cause Hearing

---

[50] *Mueller v. Auker*, 576 F.3d 979, 991-992 (9th Cir. Idaho 2009) and *Springer v. Placer County*, 338 Fed. Appx. 587, 590 (9th Cir. Cal. 2009).

BENCH CARD

Show Cause Hearing

A fair, unbiased hearing in which all parties have equal opportunity to be heard.

QUESTIONS TO ANSWER

1. Did all the parties, including the court, perform the actions enumerated in the Bench Card titled: Roles of Parties before and during hearings?
2. Was process properly served as required by law?
3. Did all the parties receive copies of the petition and review the facts alleged within it?
4. Are there any possible conflict concerns regarding the attorneys representing the parties?
5. Which parties have personally met with the child and/or with one another state's attorney, attorneys for the parents, child's attorney, CPS, temporary care provider, and GAL?
6. Are there any discovery disputes?
7. Have the parties had access to CFS assessments and/or CFS case notes?
8. What are the positions of the parties and are the parties ready to proceed?
9. Have all necessary ICWA notices been given?

RED FLAGS

1. Attorneys appointed for the parties have just received the notice of appointment and/or have not met with their clients yet.
2. No proof of service filed with the court.
3. The case is clearly one that will be governed by ICWA and no ICWA expert is present.

FINDINGS

Material Facts Presented/Admitted into Evidence:

1. **Standard of Proof/ICWA:** (Indian Child Welfare Act) 25 USC 1912:

   O Preponderance of Evidence

   - or -

   O ICWA (Clear & Convincing) applies:

O If ICWA: Testimony by a qualified ICWA expert: Serious emotional or physical damage (to child if custody continues)

O Testified to/Proven

-vs-

O Stipulated to

2. **Relief Granted:**

O Parties voluntarily acknowledged a Safety Agreement, petition dismissed

- or -

O Petition dismissed with custody granted to: _____

- or -

O TIA granted (pending Adjudication Hearing) via: _____

- or -

Probable Cause:

O Exists because: _____

(Serious Bodily Injury/Sexual Abuse/Torture/Abandonment)

O Proven by: _____

(Medical Treatment Records/Other /Siblings Involuntarily Removed/ School or Daycare Testimony/Parent Interview/Other)

- or -

O Stipulated to by parents.

3. **Family Unity/Placement:** (Child's Best Interest & Welfare)

DPHHS made reasonable efforts to avoid protective placement:

O YES

O NO

DPHHS had to

O Remove child

- vs -

O Remove perpetrator

Placement governed by DPHHS and is

O Maintained

- or -

O Changed to: _____

4. **Other:**

O Misc._____

(Immediate Services/Protection Issues/Question with Paternity)

Next Hearing:

O Adjudication Hearing set for _____ (within 90 days)

O at _____ am/pm.

Notes on Hearing:

Time Ended: _____

Mediation

INTRODUCTION:

Mediation helps the parties by bringing them together to address the issues of concern and discuss possible solutions. Mediation should be held as soon as possible, preferably before the adjudication hearing when the state has TLC. It should occur again in cases where CFS is seeking the extension of TLC and before any contested termination hearing. A qualified mediator will narrow the contested issues, which in turn minimizes court intervention.

ISSUE:

Should the parties mediate?

PARTIES AND THEIR DUTIES:

1. Attorneys for Parents: Explain potential advantages and disadvantages of mediation.
2. Ascertain whether the clients want to mediate.
3. Court: Order mediation by stipulation, by granting motion showing good cause, or sua sponte.
4. Mediator: Conduct a good faith mediation, attended by all interested parties, and submit a written report to the court in a timely manner if allowed.

CONCLUSION:

Mediation is in the best interest of all parties because it facilitates informal, non-threatening communication and allows a neutral professional to evaluate and screen the matter. It helps the parents understand the legal process and their rights. It gives the parties more time with their attorneys in a relaxed setting before a contested hearing which may spur cooperation and reduce court time.

OTHER ISSUES:

Below is an over-all list of issues and documents which a mediator can address depending on the stage of the case.
- **Child Safety:** Assist in evaluating whether the child is safe.

- **Informal Methods of Providing Safety:** Review what informal methods of providing safety were attempted and discuss reasons why they failed. If none were tried, inquire whether said programs can be used without a formal proceeding.
- **Voluntary Services Agreement:** Evaluate what voluntary services may be implemented to assist the family.
- **Safety Plan (In-Home):** Review the details of any and all safety agreements that CFS employed to try to provide safety without unnecessary trauma.
- **ICWA:** Identify whether the child qualifies as an Indian child under ICWA, and if so, that the additional ICWA requirements and procedures are understood and followed.[51]
- **Safety Plan (Out of Home):** Help the parties draft an agreement that is sufficient, feasible and sustainable to help monitor progress not only to ensure child safety but also to assess whether the child can be reunited safely with the parents.
- **Child's Placement:** Review the child's current placement and identify additional family placements or possible concurrent placements.
- **Visitation Schedule:** If the child has been removed, assist in establishing a visitation schedule that the child's parents can follow. The visitation schedule should be based on the best interest of the child and the resources available to CFS. Any disputed issues regarding visitation should be formally addressed with the court during the next hearing or by special motion.
- **Supervised Visitation Schedule:** If supervised visits are required, assist in managing the threats of danger during visitations. When possible, organize visits that allow the parent to learn or model the protective capacities of another caring adult so the parent learns techniques for improvement.
- **Event Schedule:** Help draft a schedule of events for the child (school related, sports, religion related, etc.) and whether one or both of the parents may attend.
- **Contact Schedule:** Formulate and draft a contact schedule enumerating the different means and different times the parents may contact the child (i.e., phone call, text message, email, written letter).
- **Support Team:** Draft a document that enumerates the support providers' names and specific duties of support to help the parents succeed with their treatment plans.
- **TIA vs TLC:** Discuss whether TIA or TLC is being sought and the pros and cons of each.
- **Investigation Plan:** In cases where TIA is being sought, help the parties enumerate an investigation plan that includes dates and times for the investigation to be conducted and completed.

---

[51] See *supra* note 48.

- **Help Explain the CFS Process:** Help the parties understand the acronyms and purposes and importance of CFS programs such as Family Identification Meeting, Family Group Decision Making Meetings, Foster Care Review Committee Meetings, and Treatment Team Meetings.
- **Collaboration:** Stress that all parties should interact with one another in a collaborative, positive and respectful manner. This helps identify and address legitimate safety concerns and promote an appropriate treatment plan and timely reunification.
- **Examinations and Evaluations:** Discuss the different exams and evaluations that the child should undergo before the next hearing. Discusses the different exams and evaluations that the parents need to complete before the next hearing.
- **Treatment Plan:** Enumerate specific goals and objectives to custom tailor the Treatment Plan for each parent. This helps ensure success if accepted and stipulated to, and if not, it can help CFS communicate their expectations of the parties.
- **Assistance Programs:** Discuss the many different governmental and local non-profit organizations available to assist the family.
- **Care Providers Meeting:** Help implement and facilitate a meeting of the different organizations who are helping with the parents' rehabilitation and parental training.
- **Reunification Conditions:** Discuss the conditions the parent must successfully perform before reunification may occur. This can help eliminate parental confusion about what is expected of the parent and what they must do in a timely manner which may increase the chance of reunification.[52]
- **Reunification/Transition Plan:** Plan for a gradual and safe transition for the child when he/she is reunited with the parent. This may include increased visitations and involvement by the extended family, foster parent, and GAL. The plan should identify the specific responsibilities each role member has including the frequency of when the involvement should occur.
- **Legal Rights/Attorney Representation:** Verify the parents have met with their attorneys and understand their legal rights. Help determine whether the child needs an attorney and if so, establish which party is going to move the court for the appointment.
- **Notice of Contested Hearing:** Verify that the parents' and any age appropriate child's right to a contested show cause hearing has been preserved by their attorneys filing the required notice within the statutory time period.

---

[52] American Bar Association *Child Safety Guide for Judges and Attorneys*, at 33–34.

- **Stipulations:** Help the parties reach stipulations. Stipulations entered into and filed with the court before a contested hearing can help all parties narrow the focus of evidence and reduce the number of witnesses.
- **Judicial Findings and Hearing Order:** In uncontested cases, help the parties draft proposed findings of fact and conclusions of law and a proposed order that they can submit to the court before the hearing.
- **Procedural Review:** Insure all statutory procedures and requirements are satisfied (i.e., proper service of process or publication).
- **ICPC:** Discuss the possibility of an out-of-state kinship placement when necessary, and if probable, talk with CFS about starting the ICPC procedure.
- **Permanency Plan:** Evaluate the possibility of a future permanency plan and identify whether CFS is investigating the possibility of placing the child with a noncustodial parent, kinship placement, a relative after an ICPC is initiated, guardianship, planned permanent living arrangement, long-term foster care placement or a residential care facility.
- **Guardianship, Funded vs Non-Funded:** Discuss the advantages and disadvantages of a guardianship over termination and evaluate whether said guardianship would be funded or non-funded.
- **Planned Permanent Living Arrangement:** Discuss the different reasons why a planned permanent living arrangement can be used in place of a guardianship or termination and adoption.
- **Time Frame before Termination:** Explain that CFS may have to seek termination if the child has been in foster care for 15 of the most recent 22 months.
- **Voluntary Relinquishment:** Discuss the pros and cons of voluntarily relinquishing one's parental rights and if a relinquishment will occur, assist in scheduling the required counseling. Ensure a waiver of counseling has been discussed and signed.
- **Effects of Termination:** Discuss termination of parental rights and all aspects pertaining thereto.

TIMELINE:

Mediation should be held at least ten days before a contest hearing.

REASONING/WHY IMPORTANT:

Mediation eschews the adversary setting and thereby reduces the time to identify and resolve contested issues. Mediation typically provides a more relaxed setting which helps the inexperienced attorney or new care provider.

Mediation can also help the parents feel like they are getting help rather than just being prosecuted. Mediation offers more flexible time periods than a court can, which may result in greater attendance and participation. This may increase the chance of resolving the issues of danger and need. This will then subsequently reduce the number of contested hearings and help the court reduce its System caseload.

In both contested and uncontested cases, mediation helps ensure all parties are on the same page, increases the transparency and accountability of all parties and most importantly, quickens the recovery period and reunification process. Thus, it helps CFS, the legal system and all the attorneys and GALs.

It is only a win-win, however, if the mediator is qualified and well-trained in recognizing whether the System is balanced and working properly. The mediator must be neutral and independent and able to report the findings in a timely manner if required by state law (mediation is often confidential.) The mediator must also be willing to ask tough questions, especially those that help keep the System in a working balance and hold everyone accountable for their actions or inactions.

FEEDBACK:

Mediation is beneficial to all parties and many feel it should be statutorily required by all the states. The basis for this position is that courts typically require mediation in almost all civil cases, and System cases are often civil cases by statute, so there should be no difference. In fact, in most jurisdictions mediation is required before a contested marital dissolution hearing. It should similarly be required in cases that affect the entire family, especially when termination of parental rights is a potential future outcome.

Some believe the mediator should not be involved in as many procedural issues as listed herein. This feeling stems from the position that these tasks should be performed by the individual lawyers. Others are of the opinion that the attorneys often fail to thoroughly explain procedural issues and thus the more the mediator covers the better.

All agree that a good mediator can help protect CFS by ensuring that the CPS made reasonable efforts to prevent the removal of a child and/or reunify the child with his/her parents if previously separated. A mediator can review any voluntary safety agreements as well as any case plan that specifies the efforts to reunify. The mediator can also help determine whether the out-of-home placement is the least restrictive setting available for the child, how the child's health and safety is at the time, and review the case to ensure timely progress toward reunification or whether an alternative permanent placement is being sought.

HELP AID:

Checklist: Mediation

ADDITIONAL READING:

Pre-Hearing Conference Facilitator Training Manual, January 2015, written by John L. Guinn

CHECKLIST

Mediation

Mediation benefits the entire System when attended by the parties in good faith and conducted by a qualified mediator.

Mediation was: O Stipulated to O Court ordered over objection of the parties

QUESTIONS TO ANSWER

1. Did the parties attend the mediation in good faith?
2. Was the mediator qualified to conduct the mediation?
3. Did the mediator explain to the parties their legal rights and right to attorney representation?
4. Did the mediator explain the System, judicial process and statutory timeframes?
5. Is there any chance of collaboration among the parties?
6. Is this an ICWA case?
7. Is the child safe and is the child's placement appropriate?
8. Has an appropriate visitation schedule, event schedule and/or contact schedule been drafted?
9. Were any informal methods of providing safety, like a safety agreement attempted?
10. Did the parties discuss a support team?
11. Is TIA or TLC being sought and if TIA, has an investigation plan been developed?
12. What examinations and/or evaluations has the child and/or the parents attended?
13. Is there a treatment plan?
14. Is there a transition plan, and if so, what are the conditions required for reunification?
15. Did the parties propose any stipulations?
16. Is an ICPC being completed and/or were the issues pertaining to a permanency plan discussed?
17. Is a guardianship and/or a planned permanent living arrangement being discussed?

RED FLAGS

1. One or more of the parties did not attend the mediation and had advanced knowledge thereof.

2. One or more of the parties who attended the mediation did not attend in good faith.

MEDIATION REVIEW

Mediation conducted at least ten days before next scheduled hearing.

1. **Mediator Report:** (if written reports are part of the state's mediation process)

   O Filed with the court at least five days before the next scheduled hearing.

   O Circulated to the parties at least five days before the next scheduled hearing.

2. **Next Scheduled Hearing:**

   O Is still contested and the time and date shall be maintained.

   O Is no longer contested since the parties have reached an agreement pertaining thereto.

Adjudication Hearing

INTRODUCTION:

The adjudication hearing is where all parties have the opportunity to present testimony and factual evidence about whether the child has been physically abused or neglected, psychologically abused or neglected, lacks living provisions, has been sexually abused or exploited, induced to give a false report, exposed to an unreasonable risk or abandoned and therefore should be adjudged a "youth in need of care."

ISSUE:

Whether proof of the applicable evidentiary standard exists to adjudicate the child as a youth in need of care?

PARTIES AND THEIR DUTIES:

1. The court:
   a. Conduct a fair hearing giving all parties an opportunity to be heard and equal opportunity to introduce evidence;
   b. At the conclusion of the hearing, determine whether the child is a youth in need of care based on the evidence presented;
   c. If the court finds that the child is a youth in need of care, the court should:
      i. Issue a timely order that enumerates the factual evidence resulting in CFS intervention and determines the nature and scope of the abuse and/or neglect;
      ii. Discuss the child's current placement and whether the child can be returned to his/her parents safely; and
      iii. Discuss the visitation schedule, support plans, evaluations and/or counseling that should occur before the dispositional hearing; or
   d. If the facts failed to meet the burden of proof, dismiss the petition and vacate any orders involving emergency protective services and the show cause hearing orders.
2. State's attorney: Present sufficient facts to enable CFS to address all issues to obtain the relief sought.

3. Parents' attorneys:
   a. Meet with clients and explain the procedural aspects of the hearing and possible outcomes and consequences*;
   b. Discuss the child's placement, visitation, and whether the threats and dangers listed in the petition have been eradicated;
   c. Review the court's order following the hearing to ensure that only the facts that were proven or stipulated to during the hearing are in the court's order since these are the facts that govern the development of a treatment plan and could be possible reason for future termination.
4. Child's attorney: Meet with the child and the child's care provider to explain the procedural aspects of the hearing. Talk to age-appropriate children to learn their expressed wishes and whether any child wants to testify at the hearing.
5. CFS:
   a. Inform all parties of the results of any investigations they plan on using at the hearing;
   b. Be prepared to testify to the facts witnessed and what steps can be performed to remedy the safety issues and reunify the family as quickly as possible; and
   c. If the state prevails at the hearing, prepare an individualized treatment plan.
6. GAL: Meet with the child and the child's caregiver and as many witnesses as possible and submit a written report to the court advocating what is in the child's best interest.

* Consequences of Youth in Need of Care Determination: may result in a) the corresponding report of abuse being deemed substantiated by CFS, b) inability of the parent to obtain a job in a variety of occupations involving children, and c) disclosure of information related to substantiated reports of abuse to certain employers or volunteer organizations.

CONCLUSION:

The court must make an informed decision regarding the best interest of the child, the family's life and the nature of the abuse and neglect. Since the court should only allow removal of the child if the child is at imminent risk of harm, the court should order the child be returned to his/her parents as quickly as possible after the threat of danger is controlled.

OTHER ISSUES:

1. In some states, the court should bifurcate the adjudication hearing from both the show cause hearing and dispositional hearing since hearsay and/or child victim hearsay evidence may be allowed during the show cause

hearing and/or dispositional hearing but not allowed during the adjudication hearing.

2. The court may continue the adjudication hearing upon a stipulated motion by all parties, if new evidence is discovered, for personal emergencies, and for unavoidable delays.

3. If parties stipulate to a youth in need of care designation during the adjudication hearing, the parties must identify which facts are being stipulated to, unless criminal charges based on the facts are pending or have been charged, and specifically address ICWA. These facts will guide disposition, development of a treatment plan, periodic review and possible termination.

TIMELINE:

A dispositional hearing should be set within 20 days after the adjudication order has been entered.

WHY IMPORTANT:

The adjudication hearing can be one of the most important court hearings since it establishes the criteria for reunification.

FEEDBACK:

The adjudication hearing is an emotionally charged hearing. Preparation and professionalism can help control the emotional nature of the hearing.

HELP AID:

Bench Card: Adjudication Hearing

BENCH CARD

Adjudication Hearing

The purpose is to determine whether a child is a youth in need of care. The hearing must be fair and all parties given an equal opportunity to be heard.

QUESTIONS TO ANSWER

1. Do the parents understand the case and why they are in it?
2. What was the original nature and extent of maltreatment of the child?
3. What, if any, other circumstances accompanied the child's maltreatment?
4. Do threats of danger still exist within the family (either the original dangers that prompted intervention or newly discovered ones)?
5. Is the child vulnerable to the threats of danger?
6. Can the parents protect the child without intervention?
7. Do the parents have the awareness and ability to protect the child from threats of danger?
8. Do the parents have sufficient protective capacities to manage or control the existing threats?
9. What are the parents' overall parenting skills and practices?
10. How do the parents discipline the child?
11. How are the parents managing their own lives?
12. Have the parents demonstrated a willingness to change?
13. Are the parents willing to work with CFS for a positive change?
14. How does the child function day-to-day?
15. What are the changes in parental behavior being sought by CFS?
16. Based on all the information known to date: Does CFS believe the case will most likely result in reunification or termination; and if reunification, what is CFS' expected time frame?

RED FLAGS

1. Defiant parents who continue to deny any factual basis for CFS involvement.
2. Parents voluntarily entered a safety agreement but CFS failed to provide adequate services and strategies for the parents to properly achieve success.

ADJUDICATION HEARING

(Review for ICWA determination)

Evidence Proven - Allegations Admitted/Legal Basis for Intervention/ Reasonable Efforts to Avoid Removal:

1. **Child Adjudicated as a YINC:**
   - O Proven after a contested hearing

     -or-
   - O Stipulated to pursuant to state statute

     - because -
   - O Dismissing the Petition would create a substantial risk of harm to the child or would be a detriment to the child's physical or psychological well-being

     - and -
   - O Reasonable services have been provided to the parent to prevent the removal of the child from the home or to make it possible for the child to safely return

     - or -
   - O Reasonable efforts not required pursuant to state statute (aggravated circumstances)

2. **Relief Granted:**
   - O TLC for 6 months;

     -or-
   - O Safety Agreement (with child back in the home); or
   - O Petition dismissed

3. **Child Placement:**
   - O Governed by CPS

     -and-
   - O Maintained as is

     -or-
   - O Changed to: _____

4. **Other:**
   - O Paternity
   - O Visitation
   - O Communication
   - O Placement (current/ future)
   - O Exams and evaluations

Dispositional Hearing:

O Set for _____ (within 20 days) at _____ am/pm

Notes on Hearing:

Time Ended: _____

Dispositional Hearing – Treatment Plan

INTRODUCTION:

The purposes of the dispositional hearing are for the court to approve an appropriate placement for the child, which may be temporary legal custody to CFS or to some other organization or individual. The court should also approve a custom tailored treatment plan for the parents that addresses the required areas of rehabilitation and/or parenting skills, so that upon completion, the parents will be able to care for the child safely and provide for the child's basic needs.

ISSUE:

Will the temporary placement of the child sought or stipulated to by the parties protect the child's welfare? Are the safety provisions, rehabilitation programs, and training courses in the treatment plans appropriate for each parent?

PARTIES AND THEIR DUTIES:

1. The court should:
   a. Determine the child's temporary placement (disposition) considering parental custody, noncustodial parent, kinship placement, foster parent or a foster care facility, or possibly emancipation for a child 16 years or older;
   b. Evaluate the treatment plan, and if appropriate, order the parties to complete their plan after conducting a hearing on any/all contested issues therein; and
   c. Issue a timely written order.
2. CPS:
   a. Determine the best placement for the child from among the state's statutorily enumerated options;
   b. Draft an appropriate custom tailored treatment plan that identifies the issues that resulted in abuse or neglect and then enumerates the

conditions and objectives for each issue that must be met to successfully complete the plan;

c. Distribute copies of the treatment plan to all parties at least ten days before the dispositional hearing; and

d. Attend the hearing and be prepared to explain why each criterion of the treatment plan is required in the case at hand.

3. State's Attorney:

a. Ensure that reports, investigation results, evaluation summaries and/or documents regarding possible placement of the child have been circulated to the parties at least five working days before the dispositional hearing;

b. Present evidence supporting CFS placement preference and treatment plan provisions; and

c. Whenever possible, get the signed original treatment plan from the parent's respective attorney before the hearing and file it with the court for approval.

4. Parents' Attorneys:

a. Review the plan with client and discuss its obligations and requirements and stress the importance of completing all of its requirements;

b. Draft and submit a request for changes in the plan, if need be, or have the client sign and file the acknowledged copy with the court; and

c. Be prepared to address any and all disputed requirements of the plan at the hearing.

CONCLUSION:

The court holds this procedural hearing and issues a dispositional order stating the appropriate temporary placement for the child and adopting a treatment plan for each parent found to need one. Child safety should be the court's primary focus. Each treatment plan should be tailored to the specific situation and needs of the parent.

OTHER ISSUES:

1. Child hearsay evidence is often admissible at the dispositional hearing.

2. Evaluate the noncustodial parent, if one exists, as a possible care provider. If the court places the child with the noncustodial parent, the court may dismiss the proceeding with no further obligation on the part of CFS to provide services or keep the proceeding open.

3. If the court orders the child returned home, the court should establish and/ or approve a minimum list of conditions required for continued reunification;[53]

---

[53] *Child Safety Guide*, at 34–38.

4. If the child is not returned home, the court should approve a customized:
   a. Visitation schedule that includes an adequate amount of visitation days and sets the duration of the visits and sets forth an appropriate place for the visits to occur;[54] and an
   b. Event schedule that allows the parents and child to have contact at specific functions like medical appointments, school events, extracurricular activities, and religious retreats; and a
   c. Contact schedule which the child can rely on and the parents can follow that includes other means of contact like phone calls, texts, emails, and letters.
5. The court may also order medical examinations, psychological evaluations, treatment, and/or counseling for the child.

TIMELINE:

1. The dispositional hearing should be held within 20 days after the adjudication hearing.
2. If the court did not approve the treatment plan, it should set a status or review hearing within 15 days for the purpose of reviewing a modified or amended treatment plan.
3. If the plan was approved, a status or review hearing should be set within 90 days.
4. A treatment plan should be completed before the expiration of TLC unless the court extends TLC so the plan may be finished.

WHY IMPORTANT:

The dispositional hearing may be the first hearing towards healing and rehabilitation. A properly customized treatment plan serves as a road map for the parents to follow. It shows them what is expected of them and when reunification might occur.

FEEDBACK:

A custom tailored treatment plan will help all parties in the case. One size fits all plans reduce the likelihood of success. A good treatment plan incorporates many community and governmental organizations that can also assist in promoting positive change.

HELP AID:

Bench Card: Dispositional Hearing

---

[54] *Child Safety Guide*, at 33–34.

BENCH CARD

Dispositional Hearing

The Dispositional Hearing determines the best placement for the child and whether the treatment plans should be approved and ordered by the court.

QUESTIONS TO ANSWER

1. Do any of the parties have a proposed alternate disposition for the child other than what CFS is requesting?

2. Were all reports and evaluations circulated to the parties and the court at least five working days before the hearing?

3. Does the treatment plan include specific programs that will address the required behavior change and set forth examples of what change will look like?

4. What are the parents' reactions to the plan?

RED FLAGS

1. Child placement not discussed.

2. Hearing not held within a timely manner following the adjudication hearing (typically within 20 days).

HEARING

(Hearsay evidence may be admissible depending on jurisdiction)

Material Facts Presented/Admitted into Evidence:

1. **The child was previously adjudicated as a youth in need of care on**

   ———

2. **TLC may be transferred since the court finds:**
   - O TLC was stipulated to by parents

     - or-

   - O TLC ordered by the court because:
     - O Dismissing the petition would create a substantial risk of harm to the child or would be a detriment to the child's physical or psychological well-being; and
     - O Reasonable efforts to prevent removal of the child or make it possible for the child to safely return home have been provided.

3. **TLC is granted by the court to CFS or to** _____ (for six months)

   - and -

4. **Treatment plans ordered to be completed by the court:**
   - O Mother
   - O Father #1   O Father #2   O Paramour

5. **Placement:**
   - O Controlled by CFS
   - O Maintained
   - O Changed to: _____

6. **Other:** _____

   (Conditions on Placement/Evaluations)

Additional Hearings:

   - O Status Hearing set for _____ (three months) at _____am/pm
   - O Review Hearing set for _____ (six months) at _____am/pm

Notes on Hearing:

Time Ended: _____

Status Hearing/Review Hearing

INTRODUCTION:

Status and review hearings allow the court to review the parents' progress on their treatment plans and determine whether TIA or TLC should be maintained or dismissed and address the child's placement.

ISSUE:

Are the parents progressing towards completion of their treatment plans, what issues still need to be addressed, and should the child be reunified if not at home?

PARTIES AND THEIR DUTIES:

1. Court:
   a. Conduct a hearing and inquire into the treatment plan status and case progression to date;
   b. Determine whether the safety agreement and/or visitation schedule is sufficient and modify it if necessary;
   c. Determine whether the obligations, tasks and services stated in the parents' treatment plans are being carried out and if the parents are progressing with the completion of their respective treatment plans;
   d. Determine whether the current placement of the child is appropriate and necessary or if the conditions for reunification of the child have been met if the child is not reunified;
   e. Determine whether the plans previously approved and ordered by the court are sufficient in light of any new evidence; and
   f. Discuss the parents' progress on their respective treatment plans.

2. Attorneys: Be prepared to answer the court's inquiries and address any issues of concern.

CONCLUSION:

The parties discuss, and present evidence if need be, about whether the unsafe circumstances that prompted removal of the child have been alleviated or reduced so the child can be reunified. Participants should be able to evaluate and summarize whether the case is heading toward future reunification, guardianship, or termination.[55]

OTHER ISSUES:

Discuss whether there are any additional services that should be implemented in an effort to assure child safety and/or parental rehabilitation or education.

TIMELINE:

1. The first status or review hearing should be set within 90 days of the dispositional hearing; and
2. A second status or review hearing should be set within 90 days of the first hearing.

WHY IMPORTANT:

Periodic hearings keep all parties well aware of what has been completed in the treatment plans and what still needs to be finished before the case will be dismissed. Without periodic hearings, a case may stagnate and the child may fall through the cracks. If little progress is being made, the hearing gives the parties an opportunity to address the objectives of the treatment plan and for care providers to determine if a change will result in more progress.

FEEDBACK:

Periodic hearings help keep the parties engaged in their case, but can also put additional hardship on the parents since they often have to miss or leave work to attend. Do not schedule them too frequently so they do not impose undue hardship on the parties. Do, however, schedule them so the court can stay informed about what is changing as to how the parent is managing his/her life, parenting practices and child discipline and his/her ability to protect the child.

HELP AID:

Bench Card: Status/Review Hearing

---

[55] 42 U.S.C. § 675(5)(B) and *Child Safety Guide*, at 43–44.

BENCH CARD

Status/Review Hearing

Status and review hearings determine treatment plan completion and case progress.

QUESTIONS TO ANSWER

1. Is the child still in a non-parental placement, and if so, why?
2. Are the parties proceeding reasonably toward the completion of their respective treatment plans, and if not, why not?
3. Does CFS expect this case to end with successful treatment plan completion and reunification, or does CFS expect guardianship or termination?
4. Does each party agree or disagree with CFS assessment of the case, the progress the parents have made and/or are making and the current placement of the child?
5. What other services are needed to complete the treatment plan?
6. What are the child's wishes (for children of capacity)?

RED FLAGS

1. There has been little to no cooperation by the parents to date.
2. Parties disagree with CFS statement of how the case is proceeding.

HEARING

Material Facts Presented/Admitted into Evidence:

1. **Status of the Case (TLC or TIA), is:**
   O Maintained after hearing testimony
      - or - via
   O Stipulation by the parties;
   O Status is changed to _____ by the court over objection by _____

   O _____ is terminated and the case dismissed by the court over objection by _____

2. **Current placement of the child:**

   ○ _____ Maintained as is;

   - or -

   ○ Change to _____

   - and -

Additional Hearings:

A _____ hearing set for _____ at _____/pm

Notes on Hearing:

Time Ended: _____

Extension of Temporary Legal Custody

INTRODUCTION:

A TLC extension hearing determines whether TLC should be extended to allow the parents additional time to complete their treatment plans or give the state time to prepare for a termination hearing or some other permanent placement option.

ISSUE:

Can the parents learn the necessary skills and/or change their behavior in a reasonable amount of time to demonstrate the capability to protect the child?

PARTIES AND THEIR DUTIES:

1. CPS: Draft an affidavit stating why TLC should be extended or dismissed.
2. State: File a petition to extend temporary legal custody seeking continued authority before it expires.
3. Court:
   a. Conduct a hearing, inquire into the case's progression, and determine whether the obligations, tasks, and services stated in the treatment plans are being carried out and/or if the parents are progressing toward the completion of their respective plans;
   b. If the parents are not progressing, inquire into whether the state is seeking termination;
   c. Re-examine the child's placement, the visitation schedule, the current services the child is receiving and whether any additional services should be given to the child or changes made;
   d. Address any other issues the court may be able to help resolve; and
   e. If extending TLC is justified, issue an order finding that extending TLC is in the child's best interest and:
      i. State why the child cannot be reunified; and
      ii. Identify the conditions which must be met before the child is returned home and project a likely reunification date, guardianship date or termination hearing date.

4. Attorneys: Submit evidence supporting or opposing the continuation being sought based on their legal duties and clients wishes.
5. GAL: Distribute to the parties and file a written report with the court before the hearing that advocates for what is in the child's best interest.

CONCLUSION:

This procedural hearing allows the parties to explain to the court, and present evidence if need be, about whether the parents are progressing toward completing their respective plans or if termination of their parental rights is possible based on the parent's lack of progress to date.

OTHER ISSUES:

The state should amend the petition to allow a different living arrangement if it is in the child' best interest.

TIMELINE:

1. The first extension of temporary legal custody hearing should be held within six months of the date TLC was issued.
2. If TLC is extended, the court should set a status or review hearing within 90 days.

REASONING:

The hearing to extend TLC sets the tone as to how tolerant CFS will be. Extensions are favored when sought in good faith and for good reason.

FEEDBACK:

TLC extension is often necessary since the parents are trying to change years of unsafe behavior and/or substance abuse. Six months is typically not enough time for parents with many issues to overcome and then meet the minimum standards of parenting. If the parents are sincere in their efforts to be rehabilitated or learn the required skills needed for parenting, the court should accommodate them by extending TLC.

If CFS is not actively working the case, however, the court should dismiss it. Similarly, if the parents are not actively working the case, they should be put on notice that termination of their parental rights is imminent. Either way, if the case is not progressing, the other parties including the judge must drive the bus and not let the case linger.

HELP AID:

Bench Card: Extension of TLC Hearing

BENCH CARD

Extension of TLC Hearing

Determine whether sufficient progress has been made to continue state custody and assistance.

QUESTIONS TO ANSWER

1. Is the child still in a non-parental placement, and if so, why?
2. Are the parties proceeding in a reasonable manner toward the completion of their respective treatment plans?
3. Does CFS expect this case to end with successful treatment plan completion and reunification, legal guardianship, termination or other _____?
4. Does each party agree or disagree with CFS assessment of the case, the progress the parents have made and/or are making and the current placement of the child?
5. Should the petition be amended so that a different disposition from the relief originally requested can be ordered?

RED FLAGS

1. There has been little to no activity in the case.
2. The majority of the parties disagree with CFS statement of how the case is proceeding.

HEARING

Identity why the child has not been returned home:

1. **Case is dismissed by the court**

   - or -

   O TLC is extended by the court (for six months) via:

   O Stipulation by parents

   - or -

   O Ordered by the court over objection by _____

   - and -

2. **TLC is extended by the court because it is in the child's best interest because:**

   O The parents are actively working towards the completion of their treatment plans but need additional time to finish all of the programs

   - or -

   O CFS needs additional time with which to protect the child's safety as they prepare to petition to terminate the parties' parental rights or file for a legal guardianship.

   - and -

3. **Conditions upon which, if met, the child may be returned home are:**
   _____.

   - or -

4. **A likely date by which the child may**

   O be returned home is

   - or -

   O placed for legal guardianship or adoption is _____.

   - and -

5. **Placement:**

   O Controlled by CFS

   O Maintained

   O Changed to: _____

Additional Hearings:

   O Status Hearing set for _____ (three months) at _____ am/pm

   O Review Hearing set for _____ (six months) at _____/pm

Other: _____

(Conditions on Placement/Evaluations)

Notes on Hearing:

Time Ended: _____

SECTION 13

Permanency Plan

INTRODUCTION:

The permanency plan is a document that outlines the option CFS has decided is in the child's best permanent long-term placement.

ISSUE:

Is the child's recommended permanent residential placement in the child's best interest?

PARTIES AND THEIR DUTIES:

1. All parties: Evaluate and agree on possible placement opportunities for the child if reunification will not occur, with a concurrent placement in mind, like:
   a. Noncustodial parent;
   b. Kinship placement;
   c. Out-of-state placement (via ICPC);
   d. Guardianship;
   e. Planned permanent living arrangement;
   f. Permanent adoption;
   g. Long-term foster care; and
   h. Residential care facility.
2. CFS:
   a. Draft the plan by enumerating the possible placements where the child might reside for the long term duration of the case and/or until the child reaches the age of majority, explaining the pros and cons of each. The plan should examine the reasons for excluding higher priority placement options, indicate what efforts have been made to effectuate the permanency plan for the child and set forth the steps and specific times to carry out the placement decision; and
   b. Circulate the plan to the parties.

CONCLUSION:

The parties should discuss and ultimately determine where and with whom the child will reside for the long term. If the parties cannot agree, then CFS will make the final recommended placement and file it with the court along with a request for a hearing.

OTHER ISSUES:

If reunification is not likely to occur, will a termination hearing be required or will the parents voluntarily relinquish their parental rights or agree to another permanent living arrangement?

TIMELINE:

A permanency plan should be drafted and reviewed once per year.

REASONING:

A good permanency plan helps the child by establishing a list of possible permanent living residences which in turn allows the child to know that he/she will not just be moved around from house to house. Children want and need permanency so CFS should ensure the document is drafted with integrity and accuracy. Additionally, a permanency plan is a required task for maintaining federal funding.

FEEDBACK:

CFS should spend as much time contemplating and drafting the permanency plan as any other pleading in the case, since it governs where the child will live following the close of the case. The permanency plan for some children is the first real move toward permanency and the feeling of belonging.

ADDITIONAL READING:

1. Achieving Permanency for Adolescents in Foster Care: A Guide for Legal Professions
2. Judicial Guide to Implementing the Fostering Connections to Success and Increasing Adoptions Act of 2008 (PL 110-351)

Permanency Hearing

INTRODUCTION:

The permanency hearing determines long-term placement and verifies that CFS made reasonable efforts to finalize a permanency plan for a child who has been removed from his/her home.

ISSUE:

Whether the CFS long term residential placement plan will provide the child with permanency and is in the child's best interest.

PARTIES AND THEIR DUTIES:

1. Court: Hold a hearing on cases in which reunification has not occurred and determine whether the permanency plan is in the child's best interest.
2. All Parties: Be prepared to answer the court's questions addressing issues of concern.

CONCLUSION:

This hearing is the first step toward permanency for some children.

OTHER ISSUES:

When age appropriate, the court should consult with the child regarding the proposed permanency plan.

TIMELINE:

1. CFS should submit a permanency plan to the court at least three days before the hearing on the plan;
2. A permanency hearing should be held within 30 days of a determination that reasonable efforts to provide preservation or reunification services are not necessary under state statutes or no later than 12 months after the child was adjudicated a youth in need of care or 12 months after the child's first 60 days of removal, whichever comes first, as well as every 12 months thereafter.

3. A review hearing should be set for 60 days if no other hearing is currently scheduled on the docket (relinquishment, guardianship, termination hearing).
4. The court's order should be issued within 20 days after the permanency hearing.

REASONING:

A permanency hearing is a way for the court to ensure that the child will get an appropriate place of permanency and not linger or be lost in the court system.

FEEDBACK:

This is a special hearing for a child who has been in foster care for over a year without any determination of where he/she will end up living. For this reason, the court should ensure the integrity of the permanency plan and never consider the hearing simply a procedural task to approve a boiler plate document.

HELP AID:

Bench Card: Permanency Plan Hearing

ADDITIONAL READING:

Making it Permanent—Reasonable Efforts to Finalize Permanency Plans for Foster Children, Jennifer Renne, American Bar Association.

BENCH CARD

Permanency Plan Hearing

Determine whether the permanency plan should be adopted or denied.

QUESTIONS TO ANSWER

1. Do the parties agree or disagree with the CFS suggested permanency plan, and if not, why?
2. What are the child's wishes with regard to his/her residential placement? (If old enough, the court should personally consult with the child, in an age-appropriate manner.)
3. Is the plan in the best interests of the child?
4. Has CFS made reasonable efforts to finalize the plan?
5. What, if anything, must still be done to effectuate the terms of the plan?

RED FLAGS

1. Permanency plan fails to consider where the child has been residing for the duration of the case.
2. A permanency plan has not been submitted to the court within one year.
3. Boiler plate permanency plan that does not account for case specific facts.

HEARING

Material Facts Presented/Admitted into Evidence:

1. **Status of the case is:**
   - O Reunification (has occurred/is pending)

     - or -

   - O Voluntary relinquishment (previously/pending)
     - or -

   - O Termination pending

2. **Permanency plan placement option is:**

   _____

   (Reunification/Noncustodial/Kinship/Guardianship/Planned Permanent Placement Living Arraignment/Permanent Adoption/Long-Term Foster Care/Residential Care Facility/Other)

3. **Permanency Plan is:**
   - O Adopted by stipulation
   - O Testimony of experts: _____
   - O Denied

Additional Hearing:

A _____ hearing set for _____ (three months) at _____ am/pm

Notes on Hearing:

Time Ended: _____

Hearing to Dismiss/Reunify

INTRODUCTION:

This hearing determines whether TLC should be dismissed, and if so, whether any additional voluntary services should be in place.

ISSUE:

Do the parents have the ability to protect and care for the child?

PARTIES AND THEIR DUTIES:

1. Court: Conduct a hearing and:
   a. Determine whether the obligations, tasks and requirements enumerated in the parents' plans have been successfully completed; and
   b. If completed, evaluate whether the parents can protect and care for the child.
2. Other parties: Be prepared to answer the court's questions and address any issues of concern.

CONCLUSION:

This is an opportunity for the parties to discuss and present evidence about whether the cause or causes that prompted removal of the child have been alleviated and the parents can parent safely and successfully.

OTHER ISSUES:

1. Any voluntary CFS plans in place to help the parents and/or child; and
2. Any other community services in place to help the parents and child have a successful reunification and succeed as a family.

TIMELINE:

When warranted, a hearing to dismiss should be held within 90 days of a TIA case being opened and six months of a TLC case being opened unless TLC is continued.

REASONING:

When the parents have proven that they can successfully parent, court intervention is no longer necessary. It is appropriate and necessary that CFS closes cases so they can concentrate their efforts on other open cases and/or investigating new complaints.

FEEDBACK:

A formal hearing permits the court to verify that the case is being closed for the right reason. This prevents cases from being petitioned to be closed before the parents are ready to parent without intervention and assistance. If not statutorily required in your state, the parties or the court should motion for the hearing when necessary.

HELP AID:

Bench Card: Dismissal Hearing

BENCH CARD

Dismissal Hearing

Determine whether continued court involvement is necessary.

QUESTIONS TO ANSWER

1. Do the parties agree or disagree with CFS ending its formal involvement in the matter by dismissing the petition, and why?
2. What are the child's wishes with regards to the case being dismissed (for children of capacity or through the GAL)?

RED FLAGS

1. CFS is moving to dismiss the case despite the parents having not completed a substantial part of their treatment plans.
2. CFS is moving to dismiss the case despite the parents having not parented without CFS assistance with or without a reunification plan in place.

HEARING

Material Facts Presented/Admitted into Evidence:

1. **Status of the case is:**
   - O Reunification occurred on _____ and the family is doing well;

     - and -
   - O Parents have completed a substantial portion of their respective treatment plans.

     - or -
   - O Parents have not substantially completed their respective treatment plans.

     - and -

2. **Additional Informal Safety Agreement:**
   - O Parents have entered into an informal safety agreement that addresses any and all unfinished issues and/or concerns.

3. **Order**

O Denied

O Granted, case dismissed

Notes on Hearing:

Time Ended: _____

SECTION 16

Voluntary Relinquishment Hearing

INTRODUCTION:

This hearing determines whether to accept the parent's voluntary relinquishment of his/her parental rights, and if so, whether all the statutory requirements for voluntary relinquishment have been met.

ISSUE:

Is the parent intelligently, knowingly, and voluntarily giving up his/her parental rights?

PARTIES AND THEIR DUTIES:

1. CFS: Provide relinquishment counseling for a parent who wants to voluntarily relinquish his/her parental rights.
2. State's attorney: File and circulate a petition for a relinquishment hearing.
3. Court: Hold a hearing and determine whether the:
   a. Parent is intelligently, knowingly, and voluntarily relinquishing in his/her parental rights;
   b. Parent received counseling as required by statute, or willingly waived the required counseling in writing or by testimony; and
   c. Parent has the capacity to voluntarily relinquish his/her rights and understands the full meaning of loss of rights.
4. Other parties: Be prepared to answer the court's questions and raise other issues of concern.

CONCLUSION:

Voluntary relinquishment may be appropriate when a parent knows that he/she cannot care for the child with the ability to meet minimal standards and therefore believes it is in the child's best interest for him/her to relinquish his/her parental rights.

OTHER ISSUES:

1. Is the child in a possible concurrent placement, and if not, should the placement be changed or a hearing set to revisit the issue?
2. Is a kinship guardianship possible?

TIMELINE:

A permanency plan hearing should be held within 30 days of both parents voluntarily relinquishing.

WHY IMPORTANT:

Sometimes a parent knows that he/she does not have the ability to parent and the condition preventing parenting will not change in the foreseeable future. They want to do what is best for their child so the child can be raised in a home with a feeling of permanency.

FEEDBACK:

It is better for a parent who knows that he/she does not have the ability to meet minimal parenting standards to voluntarily relinquish his/her rights rather than have the rights be terminated by the court. They can go forward knowing they did right by the child instead of having the System take the child away. A Voluntary relinquishment is only effective when the facts establish a knowing and voluntary waiver of the parent's fundamental parenting rights.

HELP AID:

Bench Card: Relinquishment Hearing

BENCH CARD

Relinquishment Hearing

Determine whether the parent intelligently, knowingly, and voluntarily relinquish parental rights.

QUESTIONS TO ANSWER

1. Is relinquishment knowing and voluntary?
2. Do the parties agree or disagree with the parent voluntarily relinquishing his/her parental rights?
3. For age appropriate children, what are their wishes?

RED FLAGS

1. A parent is relinquishing his/her parental rights to avoid paying child support.
2. The parent had almost completed all of his/her treatment plan and is relinquishing based on a relapse of behavior.

HEARING

Material Facts Presented/Admitted into Evidence:

1. **Capacity/Knowing/Voluntary. The parent:**
   O Has the mental capacity to voluntarily relinquish his/her parental rights;
      - and -
   O Is knowingly, willingly, and voluntarily relinquishing his/her parental rights;
      - and -
   O Has undergone or knowingly and willingly waived any/all relinquishment counseling.
      - and -

2. **Options for the Child:**
   O Reunification/Noncustodial/Kinship/Guardianship/Planned Permanent Placement Living Arrangement/Permanent Adoption/Long-Term Foster Care/Residential Care Facility/Other
      - and -

Next Hearing:

A _____ hearing set for _____(three months) at _____am/pm

Notes on Hearing:

Time Ended: _____

SECTION 17

Guardianship Hearing

INTRODUCTION:

The purpose of a guardianship hearing is to create a formal legal relationship between the child and his/her care provider by granting the caregiver custodial and parental rights over the child.

ISSUE:

Is the caregiver qualified to take care of the child permanently?

PARTIES AND THEIR DUTIES:

1. CFS:
   a. Determine the amount of financial subsidy, if any, the guardians may receive either from the state via the Federal government; and
   b. Draft an affidavit in support of a guardianship appointment.
2. State's attorney: Draft and file a petition for the appointment of a guardian.
3. Court: Conduct a hearing and, if appropriate, make a findings of fact, conclusions of law, and decree of guardianship awarding the legal guardian custodial powers.

CONCLUSION:

A guardianship is often a good alternative to full termination of parental rights, especially if the child is in a concurrent kinship placement. Although the birth parents lose their custodial rights and parental authority over the child, their parental rights are not terminated. This preserves their ability to petition the court to restore their parental rights later in life if their circumstances improve.

OTHER ISSUES:

1. Guardianships may be federally subsidized under Title IV-E Guardianship Assistance Program (intended for children receiving Title IV-E foster care maintenance payments).[56]

---

[56] *CFS policy manual*, sections 407-4, 302-3 and 7.

2. A guardian may pursue the consent to guardianship of the child with or without CFS financial assistance.
3. The court may revoke a guardianship and reinstate custodial rights if the birth parents petition for it and the court finds that the guardianship is no longer in the best interests of the child.
4. In some states, a GAL may file a petition for the appointment of a guardian if the GAL agrees with the court who finds at the permanency hearing that reunification of the child with the child's parents is not in the child's best interest.

TIMELINE:

A guardianship hearing can be held any time after an adjudication has been made in the matter.

WHY IMPORTANT:

A guardianship can be used to terminate CFS involvement while helping a child find permanency when neither reunification nor termination and adoption is in the best interests of the child.

FEEDBACK:

A guardianship can be a good remedy for a case especially when the child is placed in a kinship placement and the parent or parents have a healthy relationship with the care providers.

HELP AID:

Bench Card: Guardianship Hearing

ADDITIONAL READING:

Making it Work: Using the Guardianship Assistance Program (GAP) to Close the Permanency Gap for Children in Foster Care

BENCH CARD

Guardianship Hearing

Determine whether a guardianship is in the child's best interest.

QUESTIONS TO ANSWER

1. Has an adjudication occurred in the matter?
2. How long has the child lived with the potential guardian in a family setting?
3. Is the potential guardian committed to providing a long-term relationship with the child?
4. Is the guardianship in the best interest of the child?
5. Do the parties agree or disagree with the guardianship and why?
6. For children of capacity, what are their wishes?

RED FLAGS

1. Guardianship is non-funded and the guardians are people of modest means.
2. CFS is opposing the guardianship and seeking termination without an adequate explanation.

HEARING

Material Facts Presented/Admitted into Evidence:

1. **Procedural Past:**
   - O Child adjudicated a Youth in Need of Care
     - and -

2. **Reunification:**
   - O CFS made reasonable efforts to reunify child with parent;
   - O Further efforts to reunify would likely be unproductive; and
   - O Reunification would be contrary to the best interest of the child.

3. **Guardianship:**
   - O Granted by the court
     - or -
   - O Denied, b/c _____
     - and -

4. **Funding:**

   O Funded in the amount of $_____, by _____

   \- or -

   O Non-Funded

   \- and -

Next Hearing:

A _____ hearing set for _____ at _____am/pm

Notes on Hearing:

Time Ended: _____

SECTION 18

Termination of Parental Rights

INTRODUCTION:

This hearing determines whether the facts warrant termination of the fundamental constitutional right to parent are met.

ISSUE:

Does the evidence satisfy the elevated standard of proof to warrant terminating parental rights?

PARTIES AND THEIR DUTIES:

1. CPS:
   a. Evaluate the case to ensure termination complies with applicable statutory and constitutional rights including:
      i. The parent abandoned the child;
      ii. The child was a result of a rape and conviction;
      iii. The child was a victim of serious crime and/or abuse;
      iv. The child was neglected by the putative father;
      v. A failed treatment plan; or
      vi. The court previously found that reasonable efforts to reunify are not required pursuant to state statutes.
   b. Draft a petition to terminate parental rights.
2. State's attorney:
   a. File and serve the petition for termination verifying service of process meets all statutory requirements; and
   b. Prepare for the hearing.
3. Parents' attorneys: Be prepared to zealously represent the clients.
4. Court:
   a. Conduct a fair hearing in which the parents are adequately represented; and
   b. Issue a timely order.

CONCLUSION:

Child needs permanency and if the parents are unable to successfully complete a treatment plan, it is in the best interest of the child for the court to terminate the parents' parental rights.

OTHER ISSUES:

1. CFS may not have to file a petition to terminate parental rights at the end of the statutory time period, even if the steps above are satisfied, if:
    a. The child is in a kinship placement;
    b. CFS has not provided the services that were needed for a safe return; or
    c. CFS has a compelling reason not to file a termination petition.
2. Upon termination of parental rights, the court may transfer permanent legal custody of the child to:
    a. CFS;
    b. a child-placing agency; or
    c. A third party previously approved by CFS.

TIMELINE:

A review hearing should be set within 60 days if parental rights are not terminated at the conclusion of the hearing.

WHY IMPORTANT:

Sometimes parents cannot parent their child and will not complete their treatment plan, but will not voluntarily relinquish their parental rights. Therefore, termination hearings must be held. In fact, if the child has been under the physical custody of the state and in foster care for 15 months out of the most recent 22 months, it is presumed that filing for termination of parental rights is in the child's best interest.

FEEDBACK:

The attorneys representing the parents must schedule enough time to review the CFS file and prepare for the hearing. This can be a daunting task since often times a CFS file contains over 1,500 pages of documents by the time termination occurs. The number of witnesses called by the state typically varies from 5 to 25 depending on the amount of rehabilitation that was attempted. Thus, the attorneys cannot take this hearing lightly.

HELP AIDS:

Bench Card: Termination Hearing

BENCH CARD

Termination Hearing

Determine whether parental rights should be terminated.

QUESTIONS TO ANSWER

1. Do the parties agree or disagree with the termination?
2. If age appropriate, what are the child's wishes?

RED FLAGS

1. CFS is terminating on an issue which was not identified and/or addressed in the treatment plan (i.e., not giving the parent proper notice of the danger concern or allowing the parent a chance to address the issue of concern).
2. CFS is proceeding forward with termination without allowing the parent an adequate amount of time to complete the treatment plan.
3. Parent is suddenly completing the treatment plan to try to avoid termination.

HEARING

Material Facts Presented/Admitted into Evidence:

1. **Termination Hearing:**

   A. **Procedural presumption:**
      - O Child in foster care/Physical custody of state 15 of most recent 22 months.

   B. **Petition:**
      - O Sufficient grounds exist for filing Petition
      - O Child's best interest to file Petition
      - O Petition filed on: _____

   C. **Notice:** Given on _____ via _____

2. **Standard of Proof:**
   - O ICWA Applies = Beyond a Reasonable Doubt

     -vs-

   - O Clear and convincing
   - O If ICWA, expert testified that continued custody is likely to result in serious emotional or physical damage to the child.

3. **Termination Criteria:**
   - O Child adjudicated a YINC on _____;
   - O Court ordered a T/P on _____ which has not been complied with;
   - O Conduct rendering parent unfit is unlikely to change within a reasonable time; and
   - O Primary consideration to the physical, mental, and emotional conditions and needs of child.

4. **Relief Ordered:**

   Termination of Mother's Rights: O Denied   O Granted after Testimony

   Termination of Father's Rights: O Denied   O Granted after Testimony

   Reason for Termination: _____

   - O Permanent Legal Custody (PLC) of _____ granted to DPHHS

5. **Child Placement/Permanency Plan:**
   - O Calls for child to reside with/at _____, which remains the same;

     - or -
   - O The child shall begin residing at _____, immediately.

Next Hearing:

A _____ hearing set for _____ (three months) at ___ am/pm

Notes on Hearing:

Time Ended: _____

SECTION 19

Notice of Appeal/ Appealing

INTRODUCTION:

To challenge the decision of the trial judge and ask a higher court to reanalyze certain decisions that may have affected the outcome of the case.

ISSUE:

Given the applicable standards of review, are there any issues that merit appellate review?

PARTIES AND THEIR DUTIES:

1. Attorneys:
    a. Consult with client and determine whether an appeal is warranted and practical;
    b. Draft and file a notice of appeal with the court within the statutory time period; and
    c. Handle the appeal or ensure the parent is appointed an appellant attorney.

CONCLUSION:

Appeal is the only remedy if the trial court rules against the parent and the party is not willing to accept the lower court's findings. It is also the remedy if the court erred in applying the law or judging the evidence.

OTHER ISSUES:

Can the trial court's decision be stayed pending appeal?

TIMELINE:

A notice of appeal should be filed with the trial court and appellant court typically within ten days of final disposition in the matter. Appeal deadlines are strict so consult your local statutes.

WHY IMPORTANT:

Sometimes the lower court is in error. Sometimes parents just need to have the decision that they cannot parent be reinforced by a higher court.

FEEDBACK:

Appeals are an indispensable component of parents' due process rights. All parties must accept that the possibility of appeal and be prepared to preserve the record through objections.

ROLES OF PARTIES BEFORE
AND DURING HEARINGS

All parties including the court should work the case and be prepared for each and every judicial hearing. The following are suggestions on how to be best prepared. [57]

Court:

Appointment of Counsel – Ensure that an attorney has been appointed or retained by all parties. In some jurisdictions, the court, if necessary, may also appoint attorneys to represent the child and the court appointed GAL.

Child Placement/Visitation – The appropriateness of the child's current placement should be conveyed to the court by every party. When possible the court should encourage the parties to locate an appropriate kinship placement. When the child is out of the home the court should discuss the current visitation schedule and inquire about how the visitations are going.

Cooperation – Inquire into whether there has been cooperation among the parties especially in the area of continued client contact and the ongoing exchange of discovery. When differences of opinions among the parties erupt, have the parties discuss their differences while considering their rationale. If possible, help resolve the disputes so the parties can cooperate with one another again.

Voluntary Plans/Agreements – Ensure that copies of any agreements and plans like voluntary service agreements, safety plans or transition plans have been distributed to all the parties and filed with the court. Voluntary agreements and/or plans between the parents and CFS can inform the court as to what actions, if any, CFS attempted before seeking formal adjudication.

Evaluations/Investigations/Discovery – Confirm that the parties have completed the evaluations or examinations necessary for the hearing and that all parties have finished their required investigations and interviews. Make sure all relevant reports are circulated to the proper parties and inquire about any discovery disputes.

---

[57] Montana Dependency and Neglect Best Practice Manual (2013). Many suggestions were derived via collective efforts of Montana's DN work group and are enumerated in the Manual.

Propose Mediation – Inquire whether the parties will voluntarily mediate, and if not, consider setting a mandatory mediation prior to the next contested hearing. This is especially useful in cases where it appears the parties are having communication problems.

Child Reunification – Determine whether the parents want to be reunified with the child, and if so, whether the child be safely reunified with his/her parents. If not immediately, then clarify what programs or requirements still need to be completed by the parents and what supporting services need to be initiated by CFS to help eradicate any possible threats of danger to facilitate safe return.

Child Participation – If the child is not present, verify that:

- The child's GAL has met with the child and/or child's caregiver before the hearing;
- The child's attorney has met with the child and/or communicated with the child's caregiver before the hearing; and
- That an age appropriate child has received notice of his/her right to participate in the proceedings.[58]

Notice of Hearing – Inquire into whether all interested parties received notice of the hearing. This is statutorily required in some states and is best practice in every state even when not formally required since it protects the record on appeal.

CPS:

Child Safety – Ensure the child is in a safe environment and out of danger.

Child Placement – If a child has to be removed, or an out-of-home placement continued, a possible concurrent kinship placement should be sought.[59]

Rehabilitation – Emphasize the steps taken to rehabilitate and educate the parents to eliminate the known dangers and any possible future safety concerns for the child.

Reunification – Emphasize the steps taken in order to remedy the safety concerns and reunify the family as quickly as possible.

State's Attorney:

Consultation with CFS – Contact the CPS and consult about the case to ensure sufficient facts support the requested relief.

---

[58] ABA Model Act § 9(c).
[59] Montana Dependency and Neglect Best Practice Manual (2013).

Present Evidence Professionally – The attorney representing the state should not seek to destroy the parents while presenting the evidence.

Know Your Case – The state's attorney must know the alleged parental deficiencies, the child's placement, and when the state expects to achieve family unity, if at all.

Partial Admissions – If a parent only makes a partial admission, ensure the facts admitted are sufficient to enable CFS to address the issues of concern. If not, elicit more testimony and examine additional witnesses to address the relevant areas of concern.

Attorneys for the Parents:

Initial Meeting – The attorneys appointed to represent the parents should meet with their respective clients within 72 hours of the appointment.

File Notice of Contested Hearing – The attorneys appointed to represent the parents must file a request for a contested hearing within ten days of service of the initial petition.

Child Placement – Discuss the appropriateness of the child's placement at every meeting.

Collaboration – Explain the pros and cons of interacting with CFS. One advantage is it should help the parties quickly identify necessary areas of rehabilitation, safety concerns and additional parenting skills. This in turn reduces the time it takes for reunification. A disadvantage, however, is that anything said may be used against the parent especially if the parent might be facing criminal prosecution stemming from the alleged abuse or neglect.

Child's Attorney:

Meet with Child – Physically meet with the child-client, and/or his/her care provider, initially within 72 hours of the appointment. If the child is age appropriate, communicate with the child before every hearing. During the conversation, explain the nature of the proceeding in a developmentally appropriate fashion and learn the child's wishes. Maintain contact with the child and child's care provider, keep them informed about the status of the case and promptly comply with any of their reasonable requests.

When representing a non-age appropriate child, communicate with the child's care provider before every hearing. Additionally, occasionally meet with the child to observe the child and see his/her actual living conditions. Discuss the nature of the proceedings with the child's care provider and form an opinion on what is in the child's best interest.

Evaluate Capacity – Determine whether the child is capable of differentiating between right and wrong, the truth and a lie, capable of considered judgment and can convey his/her wishes in a understandable manner. If yes, the child may have capacity. An attorney should consider many factors when determining capacity, including age appropriateness.

Advocate for the Child's Expressed Wishes vs. Best Interests – For a child of capacity, the child's attorney should advocate for the child's expressed wishes. If the child lacks capacity to convey his/her wishes, inform the court and advocate for what is in the child's best interests or advocate for the child using the substituted judgment standard depending on the jurisdiction and local court statutory interpretations.[60]

Child Reunification – If the child wants to return home, evaluate whether the threats of danger to the child have been eliminated, and if so, explain to the court how the threats of danger are being controlled or eradicated.

File Notice of Contested Hearing – The child's attorney should file a request for a contested hearing if the child is age appropriate and disputes the material allegations stated therein.

Courtroom Participation by Child – For an age appropriate child, inform the child of his/her right to attend and fully participate in the proceeding. Facilitate age appropriate participation in accordance with § 9 of the ABA Model Act.[61] When a child is to attend, inform the court either in advance or when the hearing is first called. After the hearing, the attorney should always take the time to meet with the child and debrief him/her as to what occurred in the courtroom. Do not assume they understood the outcome of the hearing, even on the simplest of issues.

The child's attorney must understand there are many times and reasons why a child should not be in the courtroom. For example, some children, especially those who are placed in a new school after removal, can be teased and bullied when they return to school after the hearing (yes, typically other students know they are a foster child). So use professional judgment as an attorney and never pressure a child to attend a hearing and always respect the child's right to say no.

Conflict Determination (When Representing Siblings) – If representing multiple siblings in a single case, determine whether a conflict exists or may exist before the final adjudication of the matter. Siblings may have different wishes. When a potential conflict exists, the attorney should seek an order from the court appointing separate counsel for each child.[62]

---

[60] ABA Model Act § 3(d). As explained in the commentary, "determination of a child's best interests remains solely the province of the court. ... A lawyer should determine the child's position based on objective facts and information, not personal beliefs."

[61] ABA Model Act §§ 9(d) and (e).

[62] ABA Model Act § 3(c).

Guardian Ad Litem:

Meet with Child – Meet with the child and the child's caregiver regularly throughout the case and before every hearing. If possible, meet with them in different locations to get a comprehensive perspective of the overall living arrangement.

Investigation – Conduct an independent and comprehensive investigation by reviewing as many documents as possible and personally interviewing as many parties in the case as well as family members. Form your own opinion based on the facts.

Written Report – Draft and submit a written report to the court and distribute it to all the parties of record before every hearing. Advocate for the child's best interest, not only with placement but also with how CFS is handling the case and how the parents are accepting the assistance. A GAL report should inform the court of the present and possible future of the case as well as make suggestions to the parties working the case. Do not be afraid to voice an opinion and make specific recommendations to the court.

Be a Mentor – Do not hesitate to mentor the parents who are working hard for reunification and trying to parent. A GAL can be, and in many cases is the parent's confidant and mentor while simultaneously looking out for what is in the child's best interest. A good GAL will not only make a difference in a child's life but can also help a struggling parent succeed at becoming a good mother or father. In most cases, a well-trained GAL can help a parent with reunification more so than his/her attorney.

Remain Neutral – Remain neutral and independent with respect to any other party or agency working in the System. Do not become a mouth piece for any organization.

Child Reunification – If the threats of danger have been eliminated and the parents are ready and willing to parent, advocate to the court for the child to be reunited.

Request an Attorney – A GAL may have counsel appointed by the court in some states. This may be appropriate in cases that require greater assistance in framing and presenting the GAL's position to the court.

All Parties:

Be Prepared – Be prepared to litigate and present facts and testimony regarding: 1) contested issues; 2) disputed provisions of any plan or agreement; 3) disputed sections of any reports; 4) respond accurately to questions posed by the court; and 5) suggestions that will help address deficiencies occurring in the case.

Ensure the Accuracy of the Order – Ensure that the court's order only contains facts that were admitted to by the parents or determined to be true by the court. Read the order for accuracy and make sure it is not a boiler plate order since the facts may be used later in the development of a treatment plan and/or for possible termination.

CHILDREN IN THE COURTROOM

An age appropriate child has the right to make a decision as to whether or not he/she wants to attend a hearing.[63] The child's attorney must consider if the child is age appropriate to attend the hearing and if so, does the child have the capacity to attend? If yes, does the child want to attend and participate in the hearing or just watch?

The attorney for the child should:

a. Meet with the client before each hearing and assess how the child is doing, explain the nature of the proceeds and if the child is age appropriate, explain the child's right to attend and participate;

b. If the child attends the hearing, inform the court and arrange for in-camera testifying if allowed and appropriate, and facilitate the child's transportation to and from the hearing;

c. During the hearing, ask age appropriate questions when the child wants to be heard by the court; and

d. After the hearing, meet with the child and explain what occurred during the hearing and how the outcome of the hearing affects the child and/or the progression of the case.

Sometimes children want to attend hearings that affect their lives and the lives of their siblings. If so, it should be done with the least amount of additional trauma to the child. Reducing trauma that may result from attending a hearing starts with the child and his/her care provider making a well-informed decision about whether he/she really wants to attend.

An issue to ponder before having a child attend is whether something may happen at the hearing that is not in the best interest of the child to witness first hand. Another factor to consider is will the child be embarrassed when he/she returns to school (or whatever activity the child is missing) to attend the hearing? Additionally, if the child wants to attend but is not able to at the time and date set for the hearing, continue the hearing so the child may attend.

It's important for an age appropriate child who wants to be part of the process to have the opportunity to attend and be heard. Thus, the child's attorney and GAL, if one is appointed, should meet with the child and/or the child's care provider at least five days before each hearing. Having a voice, especially in the life of a foster child, can reduce trauma and promote healing.

In cases involving young children or those who lack capacity, the child's attorney should still meet with the client and his/her care provider before each hearing and assess how the child is doing, explain to the care provider what the nature of the proceeding will be and inquire whether the care provider would like to attend the hearing on the child's behalf. This way, a child is less likely to be hurt while in the System and/or fall through the cracks of the System.

---

[63] ABA Model Act §§ 9(d) and (e).

ICWA, ADDITIONAL REQUIREMENTS

The Indian Child Welfare Act was passed in 1978 and governs modifications to state law regarding how CFS handles cases involving American Indians. An Indian means any person who is a member of a federally recognized Indian tribe, or who is Alaskan Native and a member of a Regional Corporation defined in 1606 of title 43.[64] Thus, if the child removed from his/her parents by CFS qualifies as an Indian child under ICWA,[65] the parties and the court must abide by the following additional requirements.[66]

Sections Changes:

1. Section 2), Danger Assessment – To Remove or Not to Remove

   Emergency Removal – An Indian child may be removed but must be done in accordance with state law and:
   - such removal is necessary to prevent imminent physical damage or harm to the child;
   - the emergency placement terminates immediately when such removal is no longer necessary to prevent imminent physical damage or harm to the child, and
   - the state expeditiously initiates a child custody proceeding, transfers the Indian child to the jurisdiction of his tribe, or restores the child to his parent or Indian custodian.[67]

2. Sections 5) and 6), Drafting an Affidavit to Support a Court Petition; and Drafting and Filing a Petition with the Court

   Affidavit of CFS – The supporting affidavit should be written so it factually satisfies the elevated standard of establishing clear and convincing evidence of immediate danger.

3. Section 7), Show Cause Hearing

   Legal Standard – the legal standard is elevated to a clear and convincing level in that continued custody of the child by the parent or Indian custodian is likely to result in serious emotional or physical damage to the child.[68]

---

[64] Case notes defining Indian in Section 1903(3).

[65] The case is subject to ICWA if it involves an Indian child, defined as a child who either is enrolled in a federally recognized Indian tribe or is eligible for enrollment and is the biological child of a member of an Indian tribe. 25 USC § 1903(4).

[66] 25 USC § 1922.

[67] 25 USC § 1922.

[68] 25 USC § 1912(e).

Qualified Expert Witness – An ICWA witness must be qualified as an expert, by showing that the witness can speak to tribal-specific social and cultural norms and practices, including family organization and childrearing practices.[69]

Expert Witness Testimony – The qualified ICWA expert must testify that serious emotional or physical damage to the child will occur if the child remains in his/her pre-CFS intervention living conditions.[70]

Hearing Notification – CFS should notify the parent, Indian custodian, and Indian child's tribe of the proceeding, and the hearing cannot be held until ten days after receipt of the hearing notice.[71]

Intervention or Transfer – CFS must also determine if the Indian tribe has indicated to CFS if they intend to intervene or initiate transfer proceedings.[72]

4. Section 10) and 12), Dispositional Hearing – Treatment Plan and Extension of Temporary Legal Custody

Placement Preference – When locating an appropriate out of home placement for an Indian child, absent good cause to the contrary, preference shall be given to:[73]
- a member of the Indian child's extended family;
- a foster home licensed, approved, or specified by the Indian child's tribe;
- an Indian foster home licensed or approved by an authorized non-Indian licensing authority; or
- an institution for children approved by an Indian tribe or operated by an Indian organization which has a program suitable to meet the Indian child's needs.

The above placements are not equal, so absent good cause to the contrary, a court must place the child at the highest preferred placement possibility. ICWA does not, however, statutorily define "good cause to the contrary" but one can use the Bureau of Indian Affairs guidelines for guidance on when varying from the priority of the preferences is acceptable.[74]

Active Efforts – If child is not reunified, CFS must show that it made active efforts to provide remedial services and rehabilitative programs designed to

---

[69] *ICWA Guide* at 113. To justify a foster care placement, 25 USC § 1912(e) specifically requires a finding by an expert that "continued custody of the child by the parent or Indian custodian is likely to result in serious emotional or physical damage to the child."
[70] 25 USC § 1912(e).
[71] 25 USC § 1912(a).
[72] 25 U.SC § 1911(b).
[73] 25 USC § 1915(b).
[74] Bureau of Indian Affairs guidelines.

prevent the breakup of the Indian family and that these efforts have proved unsuccessful.[75]

5. Section 18), Termination Parental Rights – Petition/Hearing

   Legal Standard – The legal standard is elevated to "beyond a reasonable doubt" that continued custody of the child by the parent or Indian custodian is likely to result in serious emotional or physical damage to the child.[76]

Additional Reading:

Bureau of Indian Affairs (BIA), Guidelines
A Practical Guide to the Indian Child Welfare Act

---

[75] 25 USC § 1912(d).
[76] 25 USC § 1912(f).